BEGIN WITH THE PAST

BEGIN WITH THE PAST

BUILDING THE NATIONAL MUSEUM OF
AFRICAN AMERICAN HISTORY & CULTURE

MABEL O. WILSON

FOREWORD BY LONNIE G. BUNCH III

Smithsonian Books
Washington, DC

For J. Max Bond

CONTENTS

If the house is to be set in order, one cannot begin with the present; one must begin with the past.

—John Hope Franklin

FOREWORD

President Barack Obama spoke at the groundbreaking ceremony for the National Museum of African American History and Culture on February 22, 2012. Since that event, there has not been a day when I have not either driven or walked past the site. Sometimes I did it just to convince myself that progress was being made; at other moments, I visited hoping to be inspired by the comments uttered by passing tourists. Occasionally I hoped that my presence would help will into existence a completed building that would fulfill the unmet expectations and dreams of so many generations who struggled and waited for an opportunity to tell America's story on the National Mall in Washington through the prism of African American history and culture.

In the early days of this endeavor—before architects were selected—one question was asked constantly: What would the building look like? While the museum staff was beginning to wrestle with that issue, a myriad of people were not shy in sharing their thoughts: The building must be monumental and marble; it must be boldly black; it must look African; it must not look African. In every case, they said, it must not obstruct the public's view of the surrounding monuments.

We examined recent museum architecture from around the world, immersed ourselves in the language used historically by African Americans to describe their hopes and expectations, and tried to imagine which architectural elements would make our ancestors smile. Ultimately we desired an environmentally sustainable signature building that would capture the feelings of resiliency, spirituality, and communal uplift that have always been at the center of the African American experience. This building also needed to remind us that there has always been a dark presence in America, a presence that often has been overlooked or erased from history. But the building had to speak to more than one community—ultimately, it had to be a monument to both a people and a nation—while also working as a museum visited by millions. Fortunately, after an international design competition, we benefited from the skills of a team led by J. Max Bond, the dean of African American architecture, and including Philip G. Freelon and David Adjaye, the lead designer.

We are humbled by the symbolism of this museum on the National Mall. The Mall is the place where millions of visitors come to understand and revel in what it means to be an American. These visitors often grapple with ideas, issues, and subjects that they might

Aerial view looking southwest at the National Museum of African American History and Culture, the Washington Monument, and the Lincoln Memorial (*at upper right*).

explore further when they return to their communities. And the building itself is ripe with symbolic meaning. Its bronze Corona reflects the patterns and creativity that enslaved craftspeople brought to the distinctive ironwork of Charleston and New Orleans. The Corona, both subtle and spectacular, is, in essence, a homage to the fact that much of African American history is hidden in plain sight, unacknowledged and often unappreciated.

On one of the many mornings that I visited the museum site, I saw an elderly African American man staring at the nearly completed building. When I looked back at him, he was crying, so I rushed over to see if he needed help. He explained that he was simply overcome with emotion by the reality of the museum building and said that it should "help us better understand who we are as Americans and point us toward a better tomorrow." All who are involved with the creation of the National Museum of African American History and Culture hope he is right.

Lonnie G. Bunch III

FOUNDING DIRECTOR, NATIONAL MUSEUM OF AFRICAN AMERICAN HISTORY & CULTURE

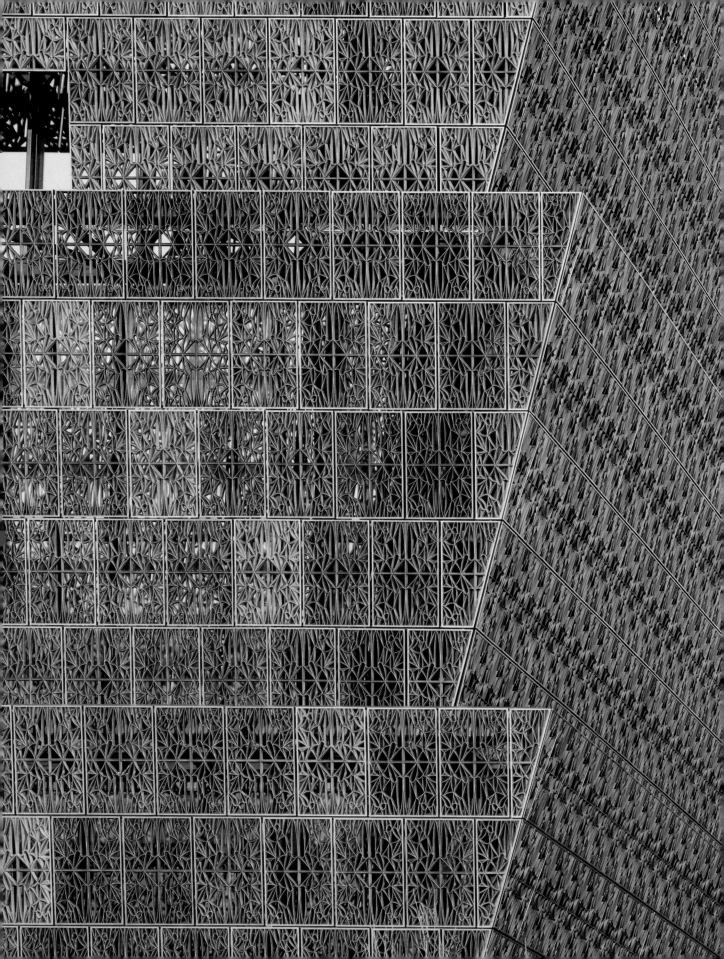

INTRODUCTION

As visitors to the National Mall walk west and draw near the Washington Monument, a new sight greets them. Rising to their right is the façade of an utterly original structure—the triple-tiered Corona of the Smithsonian National Museum of African American History and Culture. The Corona's metallic carapace shimmers reddish-gold, deep sepia, or copper in the changing light, a dazzling tribute to African American contributions to American craft and building.

It is fitting that the newest of the Mall's museums is also the closest to the Washington Monument, built to honor the first president of the United States. The Museum's proximity is a reminder of the vital role that African Americans have played in the rich and complex history of the nation. As the Museum's founding director, Lonnie G. Bunch III, has said, "You can learn a great deal about a country, about a people, by what it remembers. The Corona is a beacon that reminds us of what we were and what challenges we still face, and it points us toward what we can become."

Corner view of the Corona's three tiers. The intricate details of its bronze-colored screen panels shimmer in the late-afternoon sunlight.

The need for a national museum of African American history emerged in the early twentieth century, when demands that black contributions to the nation be publicly acknowledged gained momentum. In many ways, the story of the Museum's creation echoes black history in America. It begins with the African American insistence that America live up to the values of equal rights enshrined in the Declaration of Independence, goes on to chronicle battles against institutional racism in the celebrated halls of national heritage, and ultimately shows how Americans—museum experts, politicians, architects, philanthropists, and citizens—worked together to launch a new vision of how museums can address the difficult history of race and racism.

The Smithsonian Institution wanted to construct a building so compelling that it would attract visitors from across the globe. It had to be inventive, with space for individual reflection and state-of-the-art galleries, accessible public areas, and innovative classroom and theater spaces for collective celebration. It wanted even casual visitors, drawn by the building's unique façade, to feel compelled to walk inside and explore the meticulously curated galleries capturing the many facets, both uplifting and somber, of the African American experience.

The Museum was designed by Freelon Adjaye Bond with the Smith Group (FAB/S), a collaboration of four internationally renowned architecture firms, with David Adjaye, a New York City– and London-based architect, taking the design lead. In the best architectural tradition, elements of the design draw on both history and African American sensibilities of place to make a bold architectural statement. The Corona's distinctive look, for example, is inspired by two forms: the traditional sculptural columns found in the courtyards of West African shrines and the gesture of a group of people with arms raised in praise and jubilation. It also draws inspiration from the cast ironwork on antebellum buildings in New Orleans and Charleston. Because racism has influenced the narratives presented in American history, the artistic contributions of the enslaved and freed black men who forged such ironwork was not attributed until recently. This oversight constitutes what Director Bunch has called history "hiding in plain sight."

From the National Mall and Constitution Avenue, a colorful landscape of trees and verdant gardens welcomes visitors to the Museum grounds. Outdoor vignettes, such as the Reading Grove on the north side and a fountain inscribed with revelatory quotes from black leaders on the south, link to the history told inside the Museum. Most visitors approaching the Museum from the Mall make their way to the south Porch entrance, modeled on the porches shading the fronts of southern shotgun houses. The Porch's deep overhang provides the same cooling effect in the hot summer months that its smaller domestic cousin does. For the architect of record on the project, Philip G. Freelon, this interplay between the Porch's form and function "underscores the importance that the Museum not just be a place about and for African Americans but, as Director Bunch says, that it tell the quintessential American story. Therefore, it is important that the Museum feels open and welcoming to everyone."

Vista of the Museum from Constitution Avenue, looking across the north lawn to the Washington Monument.

The Museum's central Heritage Hall is a sweeping space with a luminous black ceiling that is lower toward the center of the space, creating a stepped, convex form. The architects envisioned the central hall as the Museum's meeting place and crossroads, a grand room that draws people into the building's center to pick up information. The ceiling then gestures visitors back to the perimeter of the space, where escalators and stairs lead

Following pages: View from the Washington Monument Grounds, looking northeast to the Museum.

Light filtering through the Corona's screen into the Community Galleries on the Museum's third level.

down to the Concourse level, and a glass elevator carries visitors down to the History Galleries or up to the Explore Your Family History installations and research centers and the Culture and Community Galleries. On all four sides of the entrance level, floor-to-ceiling windows treat visitors to views of the surrounding landscape. This outside-in design is an unusual feature; the entrance halls of most museums are surrounded by galleries.

All these design features spring from the Museum's core architectural concept—a building that Adjaye envisioned as a series of nested containers. The upper-level galleries reside in the core container, wrapped by a perimeter zone dedicated to circulation passages and enclosed by a glass curtain wall; the panels of the Corona form the exterior container. As visitors move between these layers, they discover spectacular vistas. On the lower Concourse, for example, people can look upward through several stories and see first the bridge of the north entrance, then the third-level balcony of the Community Galleries, and then skyward through the Corona's screen. Dramatic spaces like these convey a sense of uplift, according to Bunch, and instill "a spiritual feeling like that felt in a cathedral."

The galleries provide more than 100,000 square feet of exhibition space. The inventive displays weave together themes of history, culture, and community, using items selected from more than 40,000 artifacts assembled over the course of a decade. The extraordinary cache includes cherished family heirlooms donated to the Museum and historic

The Corona's west façade casting sunlight and shadows along the main perimeter zone leading to the upper galleries. Security checkpoints, escalators, the grand staircase to the Concourse level, the museum shop, and the coat- and bag-check area are also in this zone. Other functions, including elevators and other vital services, are in four large pillars in the Heritage Hall.

treasures from all over the country and the world. The diverse exhibitions, some with changing displays, take visitors along a multivoiced African American journey. Visitors hear stories of unyielding determination and triumph over seemingly insurmountable obstacles. They learn how the black struggle for equality redefined America's democratic ethos over the course of 250 years, beginning with the hard-won freedoms upheld by the Thirteenth, Fourteenth, and Fifteenth Constitutional amendments passed after the end of slavery and the Civil War to provide equal protection and voting rights for all American males, regardless of race or ethnicity.

The need for considerable space was a major factor in the decision to build 60 percent of the Museum underground. The lower-level History Galleries, which are the largest exhibition space in any Smithsonian museum, begin their narrative a full sixty-five feet underground. The team of curators divided the History Galleries into three thematic exhibitions: "Slavery and Freedom," "Defending Freedom, Defining Freedom: Era of Segregation 1876–1968," and "A Changing America: 1968 and Beyond," taking visitors on a chronological journey through dozens of multimedia galleries. Ramps connect the three exhibitions, with Landing Theaters where visitors can pause for an overview of the next theme on the route or reflect on what they have just experienced.

The exhibitions vary greatly in size. In small galleries, the low ceilings bring the story intimately close, while the large galleries soar four stories high. In one such cavernous space, the eye is drawn upward to an aircraft piloted during World War II by the famed Tuskegee airmen, the first African American pilots to serve in the armed forces. Other capacious galleries house a bounty of rare artifacts, including a segregated rail car from the 1920s and a diminutive wood-frame cabin that was once home to an enslaved family living in coastal South Carolina. In the words of Bunch, these galleries "bridge a gap in our national memory by creating exhibitions and programs focusing on a wide arc of history."

The Contemplative Court nestles above the History Galleries. Copper-inlaid glass panels enclose the chamber and bathe it in a radiant glow. In the center, the Oculus fountain drips in a wide circle into a pool below. The Contemplative Court is designed to be a hidden treasure discovered at the end of the journey through the exhibitions. It offers an interlude for reflection upon the inspiring as well as difficult and complicated stories that are not often told in museums presenting American history.

The upper-level galleries celebrate the rich complexity of African American culture. The Community Galleries, for example, a series of interconnected spaces on the third floor, describe how African Americans formed institutions and organizations to serve the needs of their communities and enact social change. Artifacts displayed in the exhibitions "Sports: Leveling the Playing Field" and "Double Victory: The African American Military Experience" highlight important arenas of black achievement and recount how African American men and women challenged segregation. The ten vignettes in the "Power of Place" exhibition take visitors into locales across the United States to show the diverse experiences of African Africans. A series of displays in "Making a Way Out of No Way" explores themes of agency, creativity, and resilience through the personal stories of African Americans who challenged racial oppression and discrimination and created ways to live with dignity and pride.

On the fourth level, a series of open-plan galleries separated by gently curving walls make up the Culture Galleries. Here, the exhibitions "Cultural Expressions," "Musical Crossroads," "Taking the Stage," and "Visual Art and the American Experience" showcase black contributions to music, film, media, theater, and the visual arts. Sound-scapes, interactive screens, and large projections enliven the viewing experience. Visitors can revel in African American culture and style while hearing stories of cultural survival, individual accomplishments, and social progress.

One of the most important goals Bunch set for the architects was to create an environmentally efficient building that would be respected worldwide. As a result, the floors, ceilings, walls, and other elements are constructed with regionally sourced and recycled materials, and the management of energy, water, and air quality takes full advantage of the local climate and context. The Corona and the Porch double as passive energy features that help make the interior and exterior environments comfortable for the public and staff year-round. It is hoped that this integrated design philosophy will help the Museum gain Gold certification from the U.S. Green Building Council's Leadership in Energy and Environmental Design (LEED) program, making it the Smithsonian's first newly constructed certified green museum.

For Bunch, the Museum's central mission is "to help all Americans remember and, by remembering, to stimulate a dialogue about race and help foster a spirit of reconciliation and healing." To embody this concept in the design, the architects incorporated Lens spaces on the upper level. These balconies and openings extend through the Corona, providing dramatic views of the nearby monuments and civic buildings. Visitors can take stock of the symbols of the nation and the sites where many of the important struggles for equality have occurred, including the West Front of the U.S. Capitol building, where the forty-fourth president of the United States, Barack Obama, was inaugurated in 2009, and the steps of the Lincoln Memorial, where singer Marian Anderson sang after being barred from performing to an integrated audience at a local concert hall in 1939. This opportunity to grapple with the nation's difficult—and at times painful—racial history moves America closer to its ideals of liberty and freedom for everyone.

What follows is the story of the making of the National Museum of African American History and Culture, from overcoming the deeply rooted prejudices and institutional challenges that stymied early initiatives to solving considerable practical problems, including funding, management, content, and location, once Congress had given the green light. It goes on to relate how the innovative building was conceived, designed, and constructed, beginning with an architectural competition, and discusses the many considerations that contributed to the decision-making process. The architecture had to embody African American cultural sensibilities about space, form, and material. But what should those be and who should decide? How should the Smithsonian National Museum of African American History and Culture proclaim its place in the nation's collective memory and claim its place on America's public commons—the National Mall?

PART 1

An African American Museum for All

In the period after the Civil War and Reconstruction, women and men began to call for the creation of institutions and landmarks to acknowledge the achievements of African Americans. Emancipation celebrations held around the country in the late 1800s and early 1900s presented ideal opportunities to make such calls. Communities sometimes held these events on the Fourth of July to coincide with the national holiday commemorating American independence and to draw attention to the contributions black Americans had made to the nation.

Black leaders often delivered uplifting speeches at the emancipation celebrations, acknowledging the great strides black Americans had made since slavery ended and emphasizing that the African American spirit embodied the resilience and fortitude celebrated by such events. The speakers praised America for promising freedom and equality for all its citizens, but also warned of the rise of new forms of racism such as the Jim Crow segregation laws that threatened progress toward equality.

African Americans marching in an Emancipation Day celebration in Richmond, Virginia, ca. 1905.

In their Grand Army of the Republic caps and uniforms, African American Civil War veterans, joined by young women, march in procession, ca. 1912.

After the Civil War, African American veterans joined fraternal organizations such as the Grand Army of the Republic (GAR), a national association of former Union Army soldiers that recognized the service of black soldiers. Local branches of the GAR dedicated monuments and memorial plaques to important Civil War figures and battles, and each year black and white members of the organization gathered to remember the sacrifices made to preserve the Union and to honor fallen soldiers and sailors. Such commemorations were eventually marked by a new national holiday, Memorial Day. African American members of fraternal orders often marched in their military uniforms at emancipation celebrations in towns across the United States. These former soldiers symbolized the dedication of all African Americans who had served and died in America's conflicts since the Revolutionary War.

Proud of their history of service and yet excluded from the lists of names engraved on mainstream monuments, African Americans campaigned for their own monuments honoring black soldiers. The abolitionist Frederick Douglass supported a monument to black soldiers in his former home of Rochester, New York. With two sons who had enlisted in the Civil War, he thought it fitting to establish a "monument in honor of the colored soldiers who, under great discouragements, at the moment of national peril volunteered to go to the front and fight for their country."

Segregation, however, made African American dreams impossible. Jim Crow laws legalized racial discrimination. They not only prevented African Americans from voting and holding political office, but also physically separated black from white citizens in any possible place where they might mingle.

In 1915, to commemorate the fiftieth anniversary of the end of the Civil War, the Colored Committee was formed to organize lodging and events to honor African American veterans attending the GAR's National Encampment in Washington, D.C. Yet Jim Crow segregation prevented the former soldiers from staying at white-owned hotels or meeting at white-only halls. Two of the leaders of the Colored Committee, the Howard University–educated lawyer Ferdinand D. Lee and the noted civic and religious leader Julia West Hamilton, realized that these noble soldiers had fought for a country that still did not recognize them as citizens.

The Colored Committee proposed that a monument honoring African American veterans of the Civil War, as well as the nation's other wars, be erected in Washington, D.C. In 1916, with the approval of the GAR, Lee, Hamilton, and others officially formed the National Association for the Erection of a Monument at the National Capital in Honor of the Negro Soldiers and Sailors Who Fought in the Wars of Our Country, which later became known as the National Memorial Association. One of the first sites proposed for the monument, according to one report, was a small plaza near Howard University.

Members of the association came to believe commemoration required more than an obelisk, however. They decided to lobby for an entire building, which could also serve as a national meeting place for African Americans because segregation put many of the public auditoriums and halls in the nation's capital out of reach. In 1916, Congressman Leonidas C. Dyer drafted a bill to erect an African American monument in the capital. The bill did not receive a hearing. But Dyer, who had sponsored important anti-lynching legislation in 1918, reintroduced the monument bill in 1919.

This time it sparked a round of discussions among the various committees overseeing federal land. In their deliberations, they raised the possibility of constructing the memorial building on the recently redesigned National Mall. These discussions were made public, but the decision to fund the project was delayed.

COLLECTING BLACK HISTORY & CULTURE

Some American institutions collected and exhibited artifacts relating to black history and culture from an early date. Black schools and universities such as Fisk, Hampton, and Atlanta initiated the first institutional efforts to assemble collections in the 1870s. As part of their mission, they began to collect rare books, historical objects, sculptures, and paintings. Private collectors made important donations to these institutions. Fisk, for instance, received a 1773 edition of Phillis Wheatley's *Poems on Various Subjects, Religious and Moral* from the estate of writer Charles Chesnutt. Because mainstream American museums at the time, including the Smithsonian Institution, did not dedicate resources to collecting African American artifacts and artworks, these universities assembled their own archives.

Visitors and students at the Hampton Institute exhibition in the Negro Building at the Atlanta Cotton States and International Exposition, 1895.

Attempts to display African American artwork and other objects to the general public began during the World's Fairs and expositions popular from the 1870s through the 1940s. These offered public platforms for the presentation of black history and culture to wide audiences of Americans and foreigners. The Negro Building at the Atlanta Cotton States and International Exposition of 1895, organized by white civic leaders, was built specifically for objects, artifacts, and artworks made by African Americans. Despite a debate about whether having a separate building for African American culture implied an acceptance of Jim Crow segregation, the exhibition attracted black and white audiences alike. At the opening ceremony, one of the key organizers, Booker T. Washington, delivered his famous "Atlanta Compromise" speech, in which he urged his fellow African Americans to be patient in their quest for social equality so soon after the end of slavery. Washington's conciliatory views pleased white leaders, who wished to keep black Americans from power and in poverty, but angered many black Americans, who wanted to fight against the racism that infiltrated all aspects of their lives.

The other great African American leader of this era, W. E. B. Du Bois, had very different ideas than Washington did. Du Bois, a founder of the National Association for the Advancement of Colored People (NAACP), asserted in the American Negro Exhibit at the Paris World's Fair in 1900 that black Americans were socially, intellectually, culturally, and morally equal to white Americans. In reality, Washington and Du Bois were much closer in their goals than their words might suggest. Du Bois favored challenge and confrontation, while Washington preferred to speak in an appealing manner as a cover for the sometimes daring initiatives he pursued. These included establishing schools for black children in rural areas where there had been none (in collaboration with philanthropist Julius Rosenwald) and raising money for legal challenges to both segregation and denial of voting rights. As for the American Negro Exhibit in Paris, Washington was involved as well, providing a rare demonstration of both men's shared goals and actions.

The success of the Negro Buildings at the World's Fairs in Charleston (1901) and Jamestown (1907) inspired African Americans to plan expositions to mark the fiftieth anniversary of emancipation in 1913. These events, large and small, were held in New York City, Atlantic City, Birmingham, Chicago, Philadelphia, and elsewhere. Exhibitions, artworks, choral performances, lectures, and pageants delighted the crowds that streamed into the great halls.

The World's Fairs and emancipation expositions lasted at most several months, so the collections were by their nature temporary. African Americans had no permanent collections in any museum. What they needed was a place with national stature where they could gather and study artifacts and present their history and culture to the public.

With this more ambitious vision in mind, the National Memorial Association hired New York City architect Edward R. Williams to design a new civic building, the National Negro Memorial, for a to-be-determined site in Washington, D.C. Around 1923,

Cast of *Star of Ethiopia* performing at the National Emancipation Exposition, New York City, 1913 (as seen in *The Crisis*, the NAACP magazine, December 1913). Activist, historian, and NAACP founder W. E. B. Du Bois wrote the pageant, which narrates the influence of African culture on world history.

Williams produced plans, perspective drawings, and a large model of the project for a public presentation. A promotional announcement sent to key individuals and organizations featured a beautiful perspective rendering and proudly stated: "Every part of this building could be used to depict some feature of historical events in which the Negro has participated."

Williams imagined a three-story granite and marble Beaux-Arts temple with a grand colonnade to welcome the public. Inside, he envisioned a national hall of fame lined with statues and busts of renowned African Americans and an auditorium that could seat five thousand visitors to host graduation ceremonies, lectures, performances, and other large events. The proposed building incorporated an extensive library with a grand reading room, and art and music rooms to hold cultural events. The *Pittsburgh Courier*, a widely read black newspaper, showcased the Williams design and

Coin bank featuring architect Edward R. Williams's design for the National Negro Memorial in Washington, D.C.

praised it as "a Great Memorial Building, not only to our living and dead heroes, but a great educational temple where statues of the great men and women of our race may be placed to give inspiration, hope and pride to the youth of our land."

The officers of the National Memorial Association, which by now included the activist and suffragette Mary Church Terrell and educator Mary McLeod Bethune, worked tirelessly for more than a decade to build support from black organizations nationwide. Historical knowledge was regarded as a way to instill racial pride and "uplift the race" out of poverty and illiteracy.

In 1928, the congressional Committee on Public Buildings and Grounds convened a hearing on a joint resolution authorizing a federal commission to develop plans for the National Negro Memorial building. The main supporter of the bill was Representative William Wood of Indiana, a white congressman. At the committee hearing, Representative James W. Taylor, a white congressman from Memphis, Tennessee, introduced Wood's resolution and responded to the committee's questions. The resolution stated that the "memorial [would] take the shape of a brick public building rather than a towering shaft or useless pile of stone." In an earnest reference to how Jim Crow segregation denied equal access to public spaces, the resolution stated that there was "no large public building in the city of Washington where public meetings may be held and where the developments of the negro [sic] race along the lines of invention and art" could be exhibited. An honest assessment of equality in principle and inequality in practice, the resolution emphasized that "so far as the Constitution is concerned, there is absolute equality; but we do know that there is absolute discrimination."

Despite negative views expressed in debates about the memorial, Congress approved the resolution and President Calvin Coolidge signed it into law in March 1929. The National Memorial Association had achieved a major part of its mission, but it still needed the funds to erect the memorial building. The cost was estimated at more than half a million dollars. This was a staggering amount, particularly because the bill required the commission to raise that amount of funding in private donations in order to receive $50,000 in federal monies. "A joker and empty honor," wrote the *Pittsburgh Courier* about the resolution's hidden terms.

Even if the sum could be raised, the memorial building still needed a location, and Washington, D.C., was deeply divided on racial lines. Building on the campus of Howard University was still a possibility. However, the enterprise was rendered moot by the Great Depression, which began seven months after the bill's signing. The economic catastrophe devastated the already precarious earnings of most African Americans, the likely donors to the museum's fund. The memorial would remain only a dream.

Poster by graphic designer Robert S. Pious for Chicago's American Negro Exposition, 1940. African Americans continued to commemorate events such as the seventy-fifth anniversary of Emancipation.

A BLACK MUSEUM MOVEMENT SPREADS ACROSS THE LAND

The National Negro Memorial was never built, but its mission to preserve and exhibit African American heritage lived on in other ways. From the 1930s through the 1990s, committed citizens and groups sought to build a national museum dedicated to sharing the African American story.

African American colleges and universities continued to collect artifacts, artworks, and rare documents for conservation and display. As early as 1915, educator Kelly Miller persuaded his friend and alumnus Jesse E. Moorland to donate his private library to Howard University. His gift of three thousand books, pamphlets, and other historical items provided such a promising beginning that in 1938 Miller proposed the opening of a National Negro Library and Museum. This proposal never materialized, but the collection was expanded substantially with Howard's 1946 purchase of the private library of bibliophile Arthur Barnett Spingarn. The Moorland-Spingarn Research Center has since become one of the world's premier archives of African American manuscripts, rare books, and artifacts.

Researchers at work at New York Public Library's Schomburg Collection at the 135th Street Branch Library, Division of Negro Literature, History, and Prints, 1938.

A similar collection was started in New York City. The Division of Negro Literature, History, and Prints opened in 1925 as a special collection of the 135th Street Branch Library. The following year, Puerto Rican–born black scholar and bibliophile Arturo Alfonso Schomburg added his personal collection of more than five thousand books, three thousand manuscripts, two thousand etchings and paintings, and several thousand pamphlets. Today, the Schomburg Center for Research in Black Culture, which forms part of the New York Public Library, is a valuable national archive and an internationally renowned center for research on the African Diaspora.

In the early 1960s, against the backdrop of growing civil rights protests and the Black Power Movement, African Americans founded public museums in Chicago, Detroit, Boston, Philadelphia, Washington, D.C., and New York. These institutions fought injustice by educating African Americans in their rich history. Their founders were equally dedicated to supporting local initiatives that guaranteed fair housing, voting rights, and equal access to education.

Artist and writer Margaret Burroughs was the first to realize the dream of founding a black history and culture museum when she opened the Ebony Museum (now the DuSable Museum of African American

Arturo Alfonso Schomburg, ca. 1896, whose collection of black writings and art grew into the world-renowned Schomburg Center for Research in Black Culture.

Artist, writer, and museum founder Margaret Burroughs (*center*) with supporters at the Ebony Museum, Chicago, in the 1960s.

History) on Chicago's South Side in 1961. A few years later in Detroit, citizens led by Dr. Charles Wright, a physician who had provided medical aid to the Freedom Riders attacked in Selma, Alabama, in 1965, formed the International Afro-American Museum. Today, this museum is known as the Charles Wright Museum of African American History and is located in Detroit's cultural center.

In the late 1960s, Margaret Burroughs and Charles Wright founded an early version of the African American Museums Association (AAMA), a national organization committed to nurturing the black museum movement. The AAMA was officially launched in 1978 by a consortium of six museums. Its dedicated founders, who established public museums in African American neighborhoods around the country, provided communities with consciousness-raising exhibitions and programs.

Founding Director John Kinard holding a rendering of the theater that was transformed into the Anacostia Neighborhood Museum, 1967.

By this time, the Smithsonian's eighth secretary, S. Dillon Ripley, influenced by the growing Civil Rights Movement, had come to believe that museums needed to take a stronger social justice approach to exhibitions and programs. The Smithsonian had documented how few African Americans and local school groups visited its museums on the Mall, suggesting that it was failing to reach black audiences in a city that in the 1960s was 70 percent African American. Spurred by the creation of regional black museums, the Smithsonian Institution opened the Anacostia Neighborhood Museum in a former theater in the poor and underserved African American area of southeast Washington, D.C., in 1966. Its first director, John Kinard, a local minister, educator, and activist, took an experimental approach to telling the story of everyday black life in the city, arguing for a new form of museum that was relevant to black audiences. Exhibitions showed the challenges of discrimination, segregation in housing, the threats of urban renewal, and the realities of poverty. Yet the Anacostia Neighborhood Museum generated a mixed reception from local community groups. Some felt the money should have been used to meet more urgent needs in the community; others welcomed the opportunity to develop a new experimental museum that explored local issues. Now called the Smithsonian Anacostia Community Museum and housed in a wonderful new complex, the museum continues its mission to examine the lives of everyday people and issues that impact urban communities.

On the heels of the Civil Rights Act (1964) and the Voting Rights Act (1965), the idea of establishing a national African American museum in Washington, D.C., resurfaced. This time, James Scheuer, a white congressman from the Bronx, New York, proposed legislation to set up a commission to look into creating such a museum. The response from African Americans was mixed. Some leaders supported the museum as an ideal vehicle to dispel myths and pave the way to better race relations; others, including Charles Wright and Margaret Burroughs, did not believe the federal government would let African Americans tell their own story. At a hearing, the writer James Baldwin said: "I think one of the stumbling blocks is that the nature of the black experience in this country does indicate something about the total American history which frightens America." Baldwin candidly stated to the federal committee: "My history is the truth about America." While the bill passed in the U.S. House of Representatives in the fall of 1968, the U.S. Senate failed to approve it, and the museum was never built.

In the early 1970s, plans for a museum resurfaced in Congress. At the same time, campaigners in Ohio were lobbying their state legislature to approve the creation of an African American museum there. In 1981, Congress approved building a national museum of black history, using private donations and involving the AAMA, in Wilberforce, Ohio, a region with a rich abolitionist history that had been active in the Underground Railroad during the later years of slavery. The National Afro-American Museum and Cultural Center opened in 1989 under the direction of historian John Fleming. The Ohio museum, however, lay hundreds of miles away from Washington, D.C.

Ohio and Congressional Black Caucus officials with founding director Dr. John E. Fleming around a model of the National Afro-American Museum and Cultural Center ca. 1988. Left to right: Henry Wilson, Senator John Glenn, John E. Fleming, Ohio State Representative C. J. McLin, Congressman Louis Stokes, Senator Howard Metzenbaum, and Congressman Kweisi Mfume.

Celebration to mark the 2003 reopening of the California African American Museum in Los Angeles. The museum was founded in 1977, and Lonnie G. Bunch III was its first curator.

By this time, other regional museums had opened or were under construction in many cities. They included New York City's Studio Museum in Harlem (1968), the African American Museum in Philadelphia (1976), Los Angeles's California African American Museum (1981), Memphis's National Civil Rights Museum (1991), and Birmingham's Civil Rights Institute (1992). But the prospect of a museum in the nation's capital remained dormant until a citizen-led coalition revived the idea in the 1980s. In a pattern that was regrettably familiar, it encountered twenty years of roadblocks, entrenched institutional racism, and disagreements about what the museum's purpose should be. Eventually, in the late 1990s, citizens, politicians, scholars, and museum professionals pooled their expertise to develop a proposal that could secure federal support to become the Smithsonian National Museum of African American History and Culture.

Entrance to the African American Museum, Philadelphia, founded in 1976.

Throughout the 1980s, amid growing popular interest in African American history, pressure grew to make public institutions such as the Smithsonian more inclusive of diverse cultures. In 1986, Mickey Leland, a Democratic representative from Texas, sponsored and successfully passed a joint resolution through Congress that supported raising an endowment for a permanent location on federal land for a building "dedicated to understanding, knowledge, opportunity, and equality for all people."

The movement to open an African American museum in Washington, D.C., was spurred in part by citizen efforts (such as those of African American businessman Tom Mack). Speaking to the *Washington Post* about his proposal to build a national African American heritage museum in Washington, D.C.—then envisioned as an American Slavery Memorial, intended to remember the lives of enslaved Africans—Leland said, "It will happen, though it is likely to take time."

View of the Smithsonian Castle, looking south from the National Mall, May 1985.

Congressman Mickey Leland (D–TX), ca. 1982, who in the mid-1980s revived efforts to build an African American museum in Washington, D.C.

After Leland's tragic death in a plane crash in 1989, Congressman John Lewis from Atlanta, Georgia, took up the reins. Lewis had served as chairman of the Student Non-Violent Coordinating Committee and taken part in a number of key civil rights protests, including those in Selma. In 1988, he had sponsored the National African American Heritage Museum and Memorial Act, which received strong support from the Congressional Black Caucus. Lewis and his staff were determined that the new museum should become a premier institution within the Smithsonian's constellation of museums on the National Mall. Lewis revived the proposal in Congress in 1989. He was joined by Senator Paul Simon, Democrat of Illinois, and this time the bill included the stipulation that the museum would become part of the Smithsonian Institution.

The Smithsonian had its own internal divisions. While some staff wanted to create a separate museum of African American history, others worried that the new museum would redirect hard-won acknowledgments of black history and culture away from the Smithsonian's extant museums of art, history, and science and technology.

This debate took place during a time of great change at the Smithsonian. Since the 1970s, the organization had been under pressure—internally from its small contingent of minority curators, administrators, and researchers, and externally from Congress and the public—to diversify its ranks. Some wondered if a new museum would relieve the Smithsonian of the responsibility to diversify its other museums.

In 1989, the National Museum of American History hired the future founding director of the National Museum of African American History and Culture, Lonnie Bunch III, as a supervising curator. After gaining a graduate degree in American history and African American history, Bunch had served as an education specialist at the National Air and Space Museum in the late 1970s, where he had pressured the institution to include more exhibitions and material about black contributions to aviation. Bunch joined historian Spencer Crew, who would become the director of the National Museum of American History in 1994, and others in seeking to increase African American, Latino, Asian, and Native American attendance to the museums. This could be done, they said, through more robust initiatives to develop inclusive public histories.

National Museum of American History • Smithsonian Institution

FIELD TO FACTORY

Afro-American Migration 1915-1940
By SPENCER R. CREW

Poster for "Field to Factory," a 1987 exhibition at the National Museum of American History focusing on the Great Migration, the movement of more than one million African Americans from the South to the North between 1915 and 1940 in search of better lives.

As more African Americans assumed key positions in the Smithsonian, the institution launched ambitious and innovative exhibitions. In 1987, the Smithsonian held the groundbreaking exhibition "Field to Factory: Afro-American Migration 1915–1940," curated by Crew for the National Museum of American History. The designers re-created sites along the Great Migration trail from South to North, including a southern farmhouse, a Philadelphia rowhouse, and an urban beauty shop, and oral histories accompanying the displays included recordings of people who had witnessed the triumphs and hardships of life in the South. The exhibition proved so popular that it ran from 1987 to 2006, and the Smithsonian curated a traveling version of it that toured widely. The Smithsonian Folkways division issued an audio documentary featuring blues and jazz music from the exhibition.

The Smithsonian took a further step to expand its audience in 1989 after a congressional bill was introduced to create the National Museum of the American Indian as a "living memorial to Native people and their traditions" out of the extensive collection that the Smithsonian already possessed. Many artifacts were repatriated to tribal communities in the process.

Yet for the Board of Regents, the Smithsonian's governing body, a new national museum of African American history raised many issues. At a congressional hearing in 1988, Secretary Robert Adams stated that the American Indian museum would take over a unique collection already in existence, but for an African American history museum, "establishing a collection that would, in fact, justify a museum is the task of a generation." In addition, John Kinard, the head of the Smithsonian Anacostia Neighborhood Museum, fought to keep the Anacostia's mission and future separate and intact. A community activist, Kinard stressed that the Smithsonian would do better to address "the man on the street," creating a vision of America that spoke to the experiences and aspirations of all black Americans.

The Board of Regents agreed to launch an institutional study. To conduct the research, they hired Claudine Brown, a seasoned museum administrator with several years' experience at the Brooklyn Museum. The proposal for a new museum within an immense institutional structure like the Smithsonian required a rigorous review of its audience, mission, policy, and operations. Brown and her staff drew together a diverse array of constituents, from politicians to community groups, and from museum experts to citizens.

The first meeting of the African American Institutional Study Advisory Committee convened in June 1990. Mary Schmidt Campbell, commissioner of cultural affairs for the city of New York, chaired the group. The Advisory Committee, composed of twenty-two scholars of African American history and culture, museum experts, business leaders, and educators, met to discuss a range of topics on three other occasions that year. The directors of the African American Museum in Philadelphia, the University Museum at Hampton University, the Schomburg Center, and other African American museums were invited to offer their perspectives on the expectations of the audience, the types and care of collections, and the struggle for resources that many black museums face.

At the first meeting, a presentation was given by Kinshasha Holman Conwill, the director of the Studio Museum in Harlem, who would later become the deputy director of the National Museum of African American History and Culture. She urged consideration of a world context for the new museum, citing growing black populations in parts of Africa and Latin America, who have been shifting the balance of power worldwide. The committee also heard presentations from the directors of major cultural institutions from across the United States. Some participants delivered impassioned calls to remember the importance of nurturing local history and institutions, which a monumental effort to establish a national museum might eclipse.

These meetings helped the commission frame the Museum's mission, shape its collecting policy and governance, and define its relationships to the public and other museums within the Smithsonian and around the country. One major issue was where in Washington, D.C., the new museum should be located. Another was the question of whether it should be a new structure or should be housed in an existing building. One possibility was the Smithsonian's Arts and Industries Building, opened in 1876 but slated for renovation. Many in the African American museum community objected to placing the museum in a refurbished building, believing that a new building centrally placed on or near the National Mall would best embody the spirit of black culture and provide a unique place to tell the African American story. These controversial and difficult questions would reemerge for founding director Bunch.

Aided by artist and scholar Deborah Willis, Claudine Brown began to identify possible donors of artifacts. Led by Willis's strong curatorial vision and her unparalleled expertise in black photography, what was now called the National African American Museum Project developed the 1994 exhibition "Imagining Families: Images and Voices" in the Arts and Industries Building. The family, an experience close to every American citizen and people the world over, was an important way to show how black American history could provide a lens onto American history in general, which was a founding principle of the new museum.

These interim efforts demonstrated firsthand that there were important histories to be told, collections and artifacts to be put on display, and audiences who yearned to know more about the black experience. Many of the exhibitions at the National Museum of African American History and Culture continue this exploration of how art and photography can serve as windows into the past and reveal how black Americans have seen themselves and their changing world.

During the 1990s, the political wrangling on the Hill continued. Lewis's persistent efforts produced another bill, which was approved in the House in 1993, yet when it moved to the Senate, Jesse Helms, a Republican senator from North Carolina, successfully stalled its progression from committee to the Senate floor. Lewis, after sponsoring the bill in every successive congressional session, finally found a Republican cosponsor in J. C. Watts, a congressman from Oklahoma, in the early 2000s. Fifteen years after Leland's first resolution, President George W. Bush signed into law the National Museum of African American History and Culture Plan for Action Presidential Commission Act of 2001. Museum supporters rejoiced at this important accomplishment, but it was the first of many major hurdles in a long process.

The law allocated three million dollars to convene a commission to research and publish a detailed report for the president. The report needed to outline an organizational structure, collections strategy, fundraising plan, and Smithsonian affiliation as well as recommend a location—and it would build upon the solid work and research of the previous advisory committee.

President George W. Bush signing H.R. 3491, which established the National Museum of African American History and Culture, December 16, 2003, with Presidential Commission members (*left to right*) Dr. Robert Wright, chairman; Renee Amoore; Vicky Bailey; Andrew McLemore Jr.; Delegate Eleanor Holmes Norton (D–DC); Senator Rick Santorum (R–PA); Michael Lomax; Congressman John Lewis (D–GA); Harold Skramstad Jr.; Barbara Franco; Robert Wilkins; Senator Sam Brownback (R–KS); Cicely Tyson; Lerone Bennett Jr.; Congressman John Larson (D–CT); Eric Sexton; Claudine Brown; Lawrence Small, Secretary of the Smithsonian Institution; and Currie Ballard.

The Plan for Action Presidential Commission spent a year refining development plans for what was now officially named the National Museum of African American History and Culture. Members of the commission—leaders in the fields of arts and culture, humanities, business, and law—were appointed by the president, senators, and representatives. Robert L. Wright, a civil rights activist and business leader, was selected to chair the commission. Claudine Brown, who was by then the art and culture director at the anti-poverty Nathan Cummings Foundation, returned to the project to serve as vice chair. Citizen members included Robert L. Wilkins, a Washington, D.C.–based lawyer and public defender, who had dedicated time and resources to studying the history of the movement to build a national museum and working closely with supporters.

To prepare the report on how the museum would serve and operate required more than the input of experts, however. Since it would be a public museum, it was critical to understand the aspirations American people had for such an institution. The commission organized a series of meetings around the country, convening in regional black museums and research centers, including the DuSable Museum, Charles Wright Museum, and Schomburg Center.

The commission completed its final report in April 2003. The findings provided a foundation for a public-private initiative to fund the construction, outlined a framework for the organization's structure, and recommended possible locations, stipulating that the new museum must be built on the Mall. The final decision to establish a new museum had yet to be made by the Smithsonian and approved by the committees that had oversight over the National Mall.

The final report emphasized the unique role the new museum would fulfill, stating that it would "give voice to the centrality of the African American experience and will make it possible for all people to understand the depth, complexity, and promise of the American experience." The commission's report laid the groundwork for Representative Lewis and Senator Sam Brownback, a Republican from Kansas, to craft legislation that would be passed in both the House and Senate chambers. On December 16, 2003, President Bush signed the act into law. Museum supporters gathered to celebrate another important milestone in the quest to build the new institution.

The Smithsonian's plans for the Museum immediately moved forward. An urgent task was to find a director who could coordinate the many aspects of the project, navigate the various approval processes, raise funds, build collections, and envision a practical concept of the Museum. This was a critical hire, and the Smithsonian carefully scrutinized candidates. Interest eventually centered on Lonnie G. Bunch III.

As a curator and administrator for the Smithsonian's National Museum of American History from 1989 to 1994, Bunch had been immersed in the Smithsonian's inner workings. He and his colleagues had shrewdly acquired the famous lunch counter from the Woolworth Five and Dime in Greensboro, North Carolina, where intrepid students had staged landmark protests in 1960 to desegregate public accommodations. Early in his career, Bunch had been a founding curator at the California African American Museum in Los Angeles. Through these experiences, he keenly understood the importance of sharing the trials and triumphs of black history and culture with diverse audiences through art, music, and interpretive history.

Bunch later became president of the Chicago Historical Society, now the Chicago History Museum, where from 2001 to 2005 he honed his leadership skills at a major organization that was expanding its mission to serve an international audience of visitors and scholars. These qualifications made Bunch an ideal candidate to build the new Museum's collections and institutional relationships. He was also well placed to advise on how to construct a unique building that would welcome audiences from around the world. The Smithsonian appointed Bunch as the founding director in March 2005.

Bunch had to reimagine the ways in which black history could reframe American history in the National Museum of African American History and Culture. He needed a powerful concept to which all Americans could relate, and one that allowed for a full exploration of the centrality of race in the country's legacy. The Museum needed a solid foundation that could be built upon by the many individuals, groups, and organizations that would join forces to create it. He drew upon his many experiences as a public historian, recalling the stories told to him by African Americans from all walks of life. He drew up a set of principles, which underwent numerous revisions in consultation with groups in and outside the Smithsonian. He based the final principles on four pillars, as articulated in the Museum's initial mission statement:

> 1. *The first [goal] is to create an opportunity for those that care about African American culture to explore and revel in this history.*

> 2. *Equally important is the opportunity to help all Americans see just how central African American history is for all of us. The museum will use African American history and culture as a lens into what it means to be an American.*

> 3. *Additionally, the museum will use African American culture as a means to help all Americans see how their stories, their histories, and their cultures are shaped and informed by international considerations—and how the struggle of African Americans has impacted freedom struggles around the world.*

> 4. *Finally, as a 21st century institution, the museum must be a place of collaboration. We must be a truly national museum that reaches beyond Washington to engage new audiences and to collaborate with the myriad of museums and educational institutions, both nationally and internationally.*

With these core concepts in place, Director Bunch turned to the next looming task: He had to secure a site for the Museum. As an historian, he had an acute sense of the importance of place as a way of telling history. The National Mall is the wellspring of the nation's collective memory, which includes an African American history that had yet to be properly represented. For Bunch, the Museum had to be "a building large enough to carry this history" and "enhance the landscape and be seen as more than an equal partner" in the compelling architecture of Washington, D.C.

The National Mall, however, had few spaces for new monuments or museums. Its illustrious two-hundred-year history as the home to monuments celebrating democratic values made it one of the most visited cultural sites in the world. To select a location for the Museum, the Plan for Action Presidential Commission visited and studied eleven sites on or next to the National Mall, as instructed by Congress, before narrowing down the preferences to five. The Smithsonian made presentations to the U.S. Commission of Fine Arts, established to vet the design of new construction in Washington's federal and historically significant districts; the National Capital Planning Commission, formed by Congress to oversee planning initiatives in the National Capital Region; and the District of Columbia Historic Preservation Office.

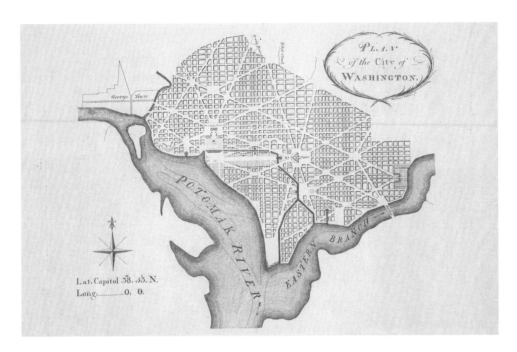

Original map of Washington, D.C., by Pierre Charles L'Enfant and Thackara & Vallance, 1792. The map shows the location of the National Mall, connecting what would become the White House, Washington Monument, and U.S. Capitol Building. L'Enfant's plan placed a civic building on what is now the Museum site.

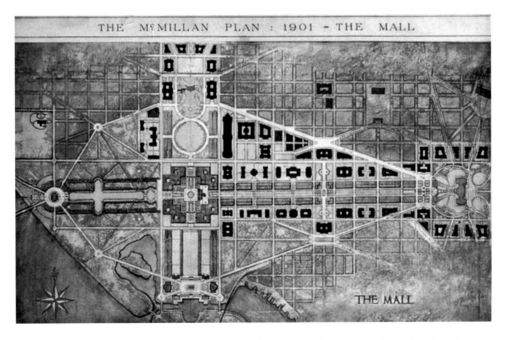

The Beaux-Arts-influenced McMillan Plan of the National Mall, 1901, for the National Planning Commission, indicating a building on the site that would become the location of the National Museum of African American History and Culture.

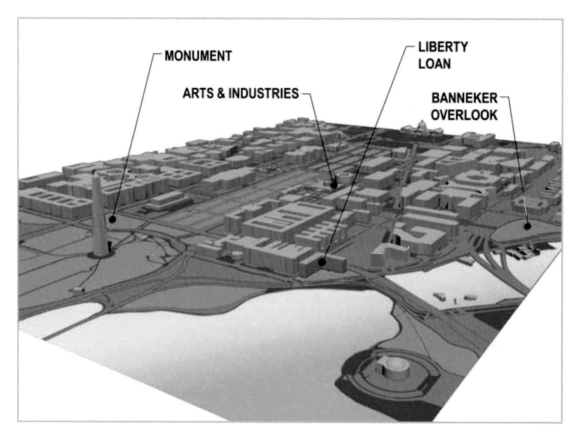

MONUMENT

ARTS & INDUSTRIES

LIBERTY
LOAN

BANNEKER
OVERLOOK

Diagram showing four possible locations for the Museum around the Monumental Core of Washington, D.C., 2005.

The Commission of Fine Arts thought the proposed site near the Washington Monument was problematic because of its exposure on four sides and the difficulty of creating easy truck access (this area formed part of the Washington Monument Grounds and fell under the control of the National Park Service). It also feared that the Museum would tower over neighboring buildings—the National Museum of American History and the Department of Commerce Building—and block views of the Washington Monument from Constitution Avenue. The National Coalition to Save Our Mall, now known as the National Mall Coalition, a group of citizens organized to preserve what they interpreted as the integrity of the Mall, also objected to the Washington Monument Grounds location. This group wanted to maintain the open space shown on the Monuments and Memorials Master Plan, a planning document for the Monumental Core of Washington, D.C., even though Pierre Charles L'Enfant's plan of the National Mall, proposed in 1791, and the McMillan Plan of 1901 both showed buildings in this location.

In January 2006, the Smithsonian rendered its selection. The Board of Regents approved the selection of the five-acre site on the southwest corner of 14th Street and Constitution Avenue NW on the Washington Monument Grounds. The board's rationale was that the locale's pristine condition made it desirable, as did its beauty and iconic placement. The National Museum of African American History and Culture finally had a home.

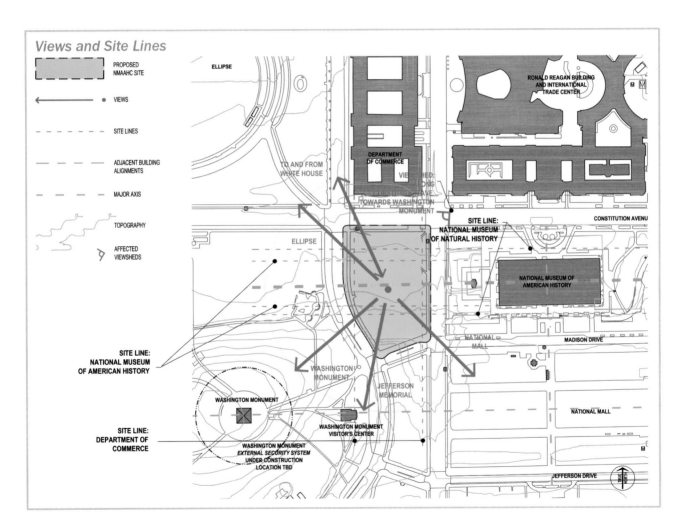

Site plan diagram identifying vistas within the five-acre site selected for the Museum by the Smithsonian's Board of Regents, 2005.

Director Lonnie Bunch and his accomplished museum team, by then joined by Deputy Director Kinshasha Holman Conwill, who brought expertise in fine arts and museum management, next had to tackle the organization of the Museum. What should the essential themes of the galleries be? The Museum had to determine its needs and goals prior to embarking upon a design direction. To accomplish this immense undertaking, Bunch assembled a team of architects, museum planners, and exhibition designers.

The first step was taken in October 2007. In response to a solicitation notice, and after evaluation of qualified candidates, the Smithsonian selected two firms with extensive museum experience: architects Max Bond, partner in Davis Brody Bond in New York City, and Philip G. Freelon, principal of the Freelon Group Associates in Durham, North Carolina. Bond was a highly regarded educator and scholar and a preeminent

Early architectural model (2009) of the National Museum of African American History and Culture by FAB/S, the team that won the Museum's design competition.

architect with an international reputation. He had built several important museum and cultural buildings, including the New York Public Library's Schomburg Center for Research in Black Culture, the Birmingham Civil Rights Institute, the Studio Museum in Harlem, and Atlanta's Martin Luther King Jr. Center for Nonviolent Social Change. Bond's firm would eventually be the architects for the National September 11 Memorial Museum in Lower Manhattan. Freelon had completed several award-winning museums, including Baltimore's Reginald F. Lewis Museum and San Francisco's Museum of the African Diaspora. Lord Cultural Resources, specialists in cultural and heritage planning, and Amaze Design, a Boston-based exhibition design firm known for its innovative approach to exhibitions, joined Freelon and Bond.

Together this team worked closely with Museum and Smithsonian staff to develop an organizational plan. Workshops with the Museum's staff helped to define their aspirations for the collection, and early in the planning Bunch and his core programmatic staff met with leading national scholars at Yale, Brown, Columbia, and Howard universities to solicit ideas and recommendations regarding content, emphasis, and the scope of exhibition narratives. These discussions were critical to building on existing theses and defining the parameters of the Museum's approach. Meanwhile, Smithsonian staff assisted with the logical order of the Museum's functions, from the most utilitarian to the most sublime spaces. It was important to capture the African American creative spirit in the face of great adversity and show how it has influenced so many aspects of American life. Conwill wanted to incorporate the artistic practices of "reclaiming, re-purposing, and reusing" to show how they provide "a through-line in African American culture, a poetic statement about how we have survived." According to Conwill, art and poetry as well as military service would reveal to the public how "black people weren't just acted upon but were active participants in their own liberation." The Museum and its exhibitions had to tell a complicated story in an engaging fashion that spoke to the human condition shared by everyone.

Two committees served, and continue to serve, in an advisory capacity to the Museum. The Museum Council, co-chaired by Richard Parsons and Linda Johnson Rice, comprises national leaders in industry, commerce, finance, politics, media, entertainment, education, and cultural institutions. Their role was to advise the Museum and the Smithsonian's Board of Regents on a range of issues, including the planning, design, and construction of the Museum, its administration, and the acquisition of objects for the collections. The Scholarly Advisory Committee was formed to help shape the Museum's intellectual agenda, exhibition content, and programming. Historian John Hope Franklin was the founding chairman from 2005 until his death in 2009.

The collective effort included studying different types of museums and institutions. Lord Cultural Resources interviewed hundreds of visitors to the National Mall to determine who would visit the new Museum and why, and what they expected to see. Public forums were hosted in Washington, D.C., New York City, Denver, Atlanta, Chicago, Los

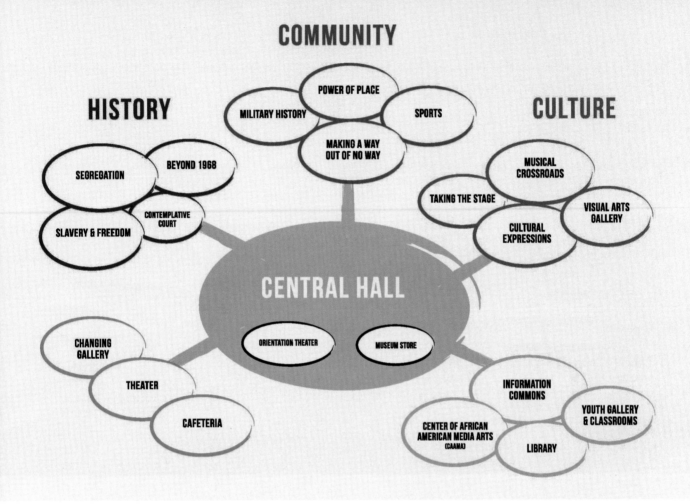

Conceptual diagram of the Museum's main galleries, facilities, and educational spaces prepared during organizational planning, 2013.

Angeles, and Birmingham, attended by more than seven hundred participants. These dialogues were critical in refining, confirming, and challenging the understanding of what the public wanted from the institution. The process also allowed the Museum to build relationships with key stakeholders and partner institutions, source artifacts, and define content.

Focus groups were asked to respond to the following questions: What would you expect to see in the Museum? Which stories must be told? How could the Museum address difficult subjects? It emerged that people wanted the curators to think beyond the borders of the United States and explore the African American experience within a global context. Many wanted the Museum "to tell the truth" and present the untold stories, the difficult and horrific dimensions of black history. It was important to celebrate and memorialize the past and to learn from those who had "made a way out of no way."

At the same time, the Freelon Bond and Smithsonian architects and engineers were developing the building program outlining requirements to house the Museum's exhibits.

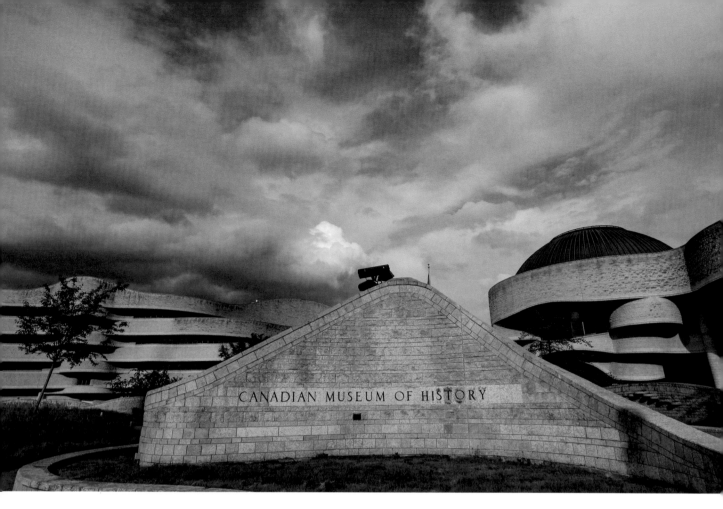

Ottawa's Canadian Museum of History, designed by Douglas Cardinal. It was among the museums visited by Museum staff and Smithsonian architects.

Once the surveys and building programming had been completed, the team compiled a seven-volume manual on how to put together the large and complex Museum. Freelon Bond and Lord Cultural Resources, working closely with the Museum's staff, spent two years developing an organizational diagram that placed the key galleries of History, Culture, and Community around a central hall. This roadmap for how to assemble a museum would be used when selecting an architectural team.

One of Director Bunch's main objectives was to deliver a museum that put ecological sustainability at the forefront of its design philosophy. The longevity of Smithsonian museums—some buildings are more than 150 years old—was a factor in this, as was the responsibility of being an institutional leader with an international audience. He aimed to achieve a Gold certification from the U.S. Green Building Council's Leadership in Energy and Environmental Design (LEED) program. Any sustainability effort is a challenging goal for a museum because of the stringent climate control and lighting requirements necessary to preserve precious artifacts. This was not an impossible standard to achieve, however, as the Museum's innovative design would demonstrate.

Bunch looked beyond the United States for inspiration. The Museum staff and Smithsonian architects, along with select members of the Museum Council and Scholarly Advisory Committee, toured museums for ideas on how a new museum could best tell its story, including places that explored histories that ran against the grain of mainstream cultural narratives. Many early exhibitions in these museums, created in the nineteenth century as national institutions dedicated to concepts of "progress and civilization," designated some racial groups as civilized and modern, while others were labeled as primitive and backward; these museums since have been updated to offer diverse historical perspectives on national histories.

One group from the Museum visited the Canadian Museum of History in Ottawa, designed by architect Douglas Cardinal, also one of the architects for the Smithsonian National Museum of the American Indian. The museum illuminates the human history of Canada by celebrating its cultural diversity, in particular giving a voice to its First Nations. They also visited the Canadian War Museum, whose exhibitions emphasize the human experience of war.

Another group visited the Yad Vashem Holocaust History Museum in Israel, a dramatically situated, prism-like structure designed by Moshe Safdie. Dedicated to research, documentation, and education, it wrestles with the public presentation of difficult memories and moving stories collected from individual experiences of the Holocaust.

Entrance to Yad Vashem Holocaust History Museum, Jerusalem, Israel, designed by Moshe Safdie. The museum's narration of difficult yet essential history was instructive for the design of the National Museum of African American History and Culture.

Early-evening view of the United States Holocaust Memorial Museum, Washington, D.C., designed by Pei Cobb Freed & Partners. It sits a few blocks south of the National Museum of African American History and Culture.

Bunch himself visited the Museum of New Zealand Te Papa Tongarewa, an institution formed out of the country's Colonial Museum and National Art Gallery, to see firsthand how an institution explores complex, intertwined narratives of place and cultural identity—in this instance how both the Maori and British experiences have contributed to New Zealand's history—and how architecture can help. The brilliantly conceived United States Holocaust Memorial Museum, designed by architects Pei Cobb Freed & Partners, around the corner from the National Museum of African American History and Culture, was another influence. It gave Bunch a sense that "you could take people on a journey" in a new way that is different from the usual shuffle past glass display cases and wall texts. The abstract architecture's subtle allusions to the history of the Holocaust viscerally stir visitors' emotions.

The next stage in the process was to find a team of architects for the Museum. The Museum's staff worked with the Board of Regents and the Smithsonian's Office of Programming Design and Construction to organize an international architectural competition, which Bunch believed would generate the expertise necessary to build a preeminent museum of considerable size on a challenging site. It also made the selection process transparent and public. In the summer of 2008, the Smithsonian issued a request for qualifications, inviting interested architects from around the world to assemble teams of architects, landscape architects, historical and cultural consultants, engineers, and a host of other consultants, from food service to security experts, and submit their qualifications. Bunch wanted to make sure that minority architects and architectural practices were represented in the pool. From the twenty-two responses, the Smithsonian selected six teams to participate in a competition to develop a concept design of the Museum.

Those six teams included top architectural practices that had designed some of the world's most celebrated and innovative buildings. Two of the architects had won the prestigious Pritzker Architecture Prize; three had won the Gold Medal from the American Institute of Architects (AIA). All of the teams had minority principals, and four firms were members of the National Organization of Minority Architects (NOMA). The teams included Diller Scofidio + Renfro, architects of Manhattan's High Line park and the redesigned campus of Lincoln Center for the Performing Arts, which collaborated with landscape architects Hood Design, the design practice Studio Sixten, and the local architects KlingStubbins. The firm Pei Cobb Freed & Partners, architects of the National Gallery of Art's East Wing as well as the Holocaust Museum, partnered with Devrouax & Purnell Architects and Planners, whose work includes the Washington Convention Center and the Washington Nationals' new stadium.

Other finalists were the London-based Foster + Partners, designers of the Kogod Courtyard enclosure of the Donald W. Reynolds Center for American Art and Portraiture, which houses the Smithsonian American Art Museum and National Portrait Gallery, and Washington, D.C.–based Moody Nolan Architects, which teamed with Antoine Predock Architect of Phoenix, Arizona. The office of Moshe Safdie and Associates, architects of Yad Vashem, worked with Sulton Campbell Britt & Associates, based in Baltimore.

The architects of the programming document, Philip Freelon and Max Bond, teamed with a young architect from London, David Adjaye, designer of the Museum of Contemporary Art in Denver and Oslo's Nobel Peace Centre. The SmithGroup architects and landscape architect Kathryn Gustafson (who had designed the landscape for the Smithsonian's Kogod Courtyard as well as the Diana, Princess of Wales Memorial Fountain in London's Hyde Park) joined Freelon Adjaye Bond to form the FAB/S design team.

In January 2009, the six finalists met at the Smithsonian for a briefing from Bunch, Conwill, and other key Smithsonian staff. The teams had two months to develop a design concept for a 350,000-square-foot structure on the five-acre site adjacent to the Washington Monument and National Museum of American History, based on a summary of the seven-volume programming document. The proposed designs had to keep construction below the stipulated budget.

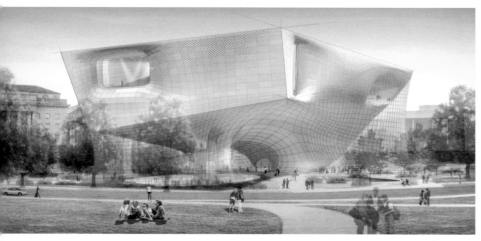

DILLER SCOFIDIO + RENFRO

FOSTER + PARTNERS

DEVROUAX PURNELL ARCHITECTS AND PLANNERS
& PEI COBB FREED & PARTNERS

MOODY NOLAN ARCHITECTS & ANTOINE PREDOCK ARCHITECT

MOSHE SAFDIE AND ASSOCIATES & SULTON CAMPBELL BRITT & ASSOCIATES

Renderings of proposed designs for the National Museum of African American History and Culture by the international teams of architects selected for the competition in 2009. Each firm has built award-winning museums around the world.

Public announcement of the winning design team, April 2009. The group includes architect Hal Davis, architect Peter Cook, Founding Director Lonnie G. Bunch III, design architect David Adjaye, architect of record Philip Freelon, Secretary of the Smithsonian G. Wayne Clough, Deputy Director Kinshasha Holman Conwill, OFEO Deputy Director for Operations Sheryl Kolasinski, and Acting Provost Richard Kurin.

The teams took a wide range of approaches. The Diller Scofidio + Renfro team proposed a glass-and-stone "cloud" that dematerialized the classical white marble museum represented on the National Mall. In their scheme, the Culture and Community galleries formed a core wrapped by the History Galleries, which stepped upward, celebrating the perseverance of African American culture.

Foster + Partners envisioned a spiral form in which the History Galleries were belowground and the Culture Galleries above, with gardens on all sides. Moody Nolan Architects and Antoine Predock Architect imagined the Museum as a rock split apart to reveal a dynamic interior. Their organic design suggested the roots of black culture and the journeys that African Americans have taken in the United States.

Devrouax Purnell Architects and Planners' and Pei Cobb Freed & Partners' monumental scheme created a wavy glass structure reminiscent of a quilt, its curves folded beneath a seven-story granite and limestone structure. A towering ship, with natural light illuminating a passage through galleries and public overlooks, was the central motif of the design proposed by Moshe Safdie and Associates and Sulton Campbell Britt & Associates.

Architect J. Max Bond (2001). A partner in Davis Brody Bond, he led the Museum's initial conceptual design and the formation of FAB/S, the team that carried it out.

The FAB/S team created an exuberant tiered form sheathed by a bronze corona reaching toward the sky. Their design drew from the cultural practices of the African Diaspora, weaving together powerful references to black traditions of building and craft. The gardens emphasized the importance of the land, their pathways symbolizing the journeys that African Americans have taken, from the Middle Passage across the Atlantic to the Great Migration northward.

Bunch chaired the competition jury, which included members of the Museum Council, publishing executive Linda Johnson Rice, and businessmen Franklin Raines and James Johnson. Also joining the jury were philanthropist and Smithsonian regent Robert Kogod, *Boston Globe* architectural critic Robert Campbell, National Endowment for the Arts Director of Design Maurice Cox, and Dean of the MIT School of Architecture Adèle Santos. The mandate of the jury was to select a team that would guide the process of building the new Museum rather than to pick a winning design. The entry drawings and models went on public view at the Smithsonian Castle, in line with Bunch's desire to keep the selection process transparent. The public was able to share its thoughts about the designs and learn about the new Museum's mission.

After hearing presentations from all six teams and deliberating for several weeks, the Smithsonian announced the jury's choice in April 2009 to an eager international audience. Secretary of the Smithsonian G. Wayne Clough stated in his remarks that the new Museum, in the historic context of the National Mall, "will tell an important part of the American story, of triumph and tragedy but above all proof of what it means to be an American," as "an ongoing story and a conversation." Bunch stated that from the start the initiative had been the work of numerous people and that the Smithsonian wanted "a team that would not lose that spirit of collaboration."

With that in mind, the Smithsonian selected the FAB/S team to develop their design. "At its best, architecture is the physical manifestation of a culture's highest ideals," the FAB/S team stated. "The National Museum of African American History and Culture— the institution and the building—embodies the African American spirit. Majestic yet exuberant. Dignified yet triumphant. Of the African Diaspora yet distinctly African American. The NMAAHC will be a building worthy of the Museum's vision—and its prominent place on the National Mall."

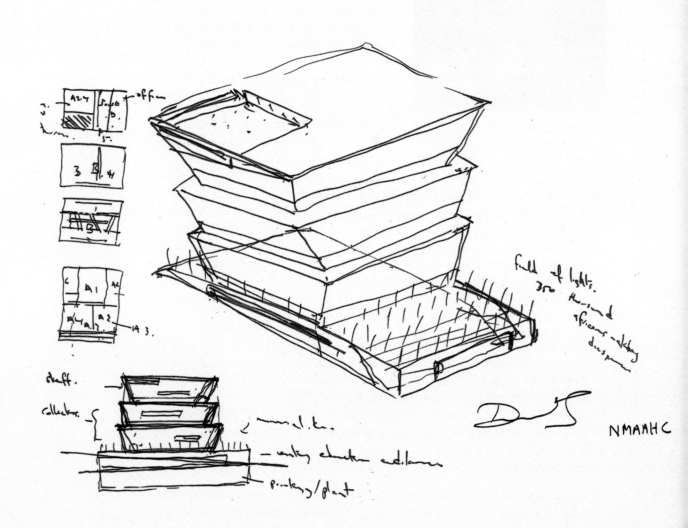

NMAAHC

CHAPTER 4
ARCHITECTURE
TELLS STORIES

Each architect and firm in the FAB/S consortium played a distinct and complementary role in the design process, which they described as working together like a jazz quartet. In the early phases, the senior member of the team, Max Bond, a trail-blazing architect steeped in the Modernist tradition, coordinated the key players. Bond's firm, Davis Brody Bond, was the guarantor of the project as the architect of record, ensuring the project would be delivered on time and within budget.

Rather than compete for the future project, Davis Brody Bond and Freelon Group Associates strategically joined forces in the programming phase and had planned to continue the partnership through the design stage. Philip G. Freelon, an award-winning architect of geometrically inspired designs, set the framework and pace for the team's collaboration. Freelon's expertise in museum design, with a number of African American museums in his portfolio, led his firm to take on the role of coordinating the design with the construction process, and the Freelon Group eventually took on the role of architect of record.

Early conceptual sketch of the Museum's Corona by design architect David Adjaye, 2009. "Field of lights," reads a marginal note.

David Adjaye, an innovative architect based in London and New York City, contacted Bond about collaborating on the once-in-a-lifetime museum competition. Bond and Freelon admired the cutting-edge talents of Adjaye, who joined the team as the lead design architect. Adjaye, whose work included collaborations with major artists such as Chris Ofili and Olafur Eliasson, had completed two major civic projects in London: two Idea Stores, which reinvigorated the well-worn model of the public library by transforming it into a dynamic neighborhood center. His refined Modernist design for Denver's Museum of Contemporary Art gave him experience with the needs of modern museum buildings and their public. Kathryn Gustafson, who had worked on the landscaping with FAB/S at the competition stage, took charge of the landscape design, an important factor in how well the museum would sit in the context of Washington, D.C., and the National Mall.

To round out the talent pool, the team needed a steady partner with experience in Washington's processes for review and approval. Bond contacted Hal Davis of SmithGroup, one of the largest architectural firms in the country, which had worked on several major projects for the Smithsonian Institution, including the National Museum of the American Indian. SmithGroup would help the Smithsonian shepherd the building through the review process, drawing on its experience in working with the Smithsonian's Office of Programming, Design, and Construction and the various regulatory committees that oversee the National Mall and the Washington Monument Grounds. For extensive experience in designing sustainable Leadership in Energy and Environmental Design (LEED)–certified buildings, the team recruited the consulting services of the Rocky Mountain Institute, an internationally recognized firm and pioneer in sustainability that had participated in the initial programming of the building.

Completing the team were the structural engineering firms Guy Nordenson and Associates and Robert Silman Associates, both experienced in developing innovative structures for world-renowned building projects, and the WSP Group, a mechanical, electrical, plumbing, and fire protection engineering firm with extensive experience in sustainable design. The structural engineers provided guidance in devising a system that would be integral to the design; the mechanical engineers ensured the outcome of an energy-conscious and environmentally sound building. The ensemble proved to be a tight-knit and productive collaboration.

The first thing to determine was what the Museum would look like and how it would function. Freelon recalls that Bond "believed that the building should participate in the storytelling and should have a hand in expressing the mission and vision of the institution." But how can a building's form capture these thoughts and emotions? How can a building's structure, and how people experience its interior and exterior spaces, tell a story?

Freelon and Bond had learned from the programming research that any design had to tell the African American journey as an American story. The design had to celebrate black creativity and mine its historical and cultural links to the African continent. Its architectural form had to capture a sense of dignity and determination in the face of seemingly insurmountable adversity.

The FAB/S concept drew upon African American and West African forms to create a two-tiered structure, with a series of main gallery and public spaces nested one inside the other. The team was excited by this design direction because it captured the uplifting spirit the Museum wanted to project. When team leader Bond passed away unexpectedly in February 2009, the team was all the more determined to carry out his creative spirit and vision.

Once the FAB/S team was under contract, it worked closely with the curators and the Smithsonian's architects and engineers to develop alternative schemes of its winning design concept. Many regulatory agencies, including the Commission of Fine Arts, the National Capital Planning Committee, the Advisory Council on Historic Preservation, and the District of Columbia's Historic Preservation Office, had to review the designs, which went through several phases of revision and refinement. A robust consultation process of more than thirty meetings in a five-year period engaged the public and agencies in the fine-tuning of many design elements. Director Bunch's strategy for these review meetings was to be as transparent as possible about the design and its intent. Bunch was amenable to suggestions made to improve the building but resisted changes that did not enhance his concept of the overall design. The three design elements that embodied the spirit of the Museum, in Bunch's view, were the Corona, the Porch, and the building's rich material palette.

FAB/S's flexible design strategy allowed for revision and variation at many points in the process. The regulatory bodies wanted to make sure that the new addition to the area respected the sightlines of other museums on the Mall as well as the important setbacks established by the McMillan Plan along the Mall, so the architectural team was asked to adhere to these prescriptions and to height limitations to allow for better views of the Washington Monument from Constitution Avenue. This determined the position of the building on the site and allowed the footprint of the Museum to form a 210-by-210-foot square. As a result of these changes, the two-tiered Corona became a more gracefully proportioned three-tiered structure and the building a small pavilion resting on a field of green (see page 67).

Time was of the essence to meet the deadlines established by the founding director, and construction needed to move quickly. To get the project started, the Museum chose to begin the construction before the architectural team had completed the design and construction documentation. In addition, a construction management team had to assume an advisory role early in the project. To complete this complex task, the Smithsonian

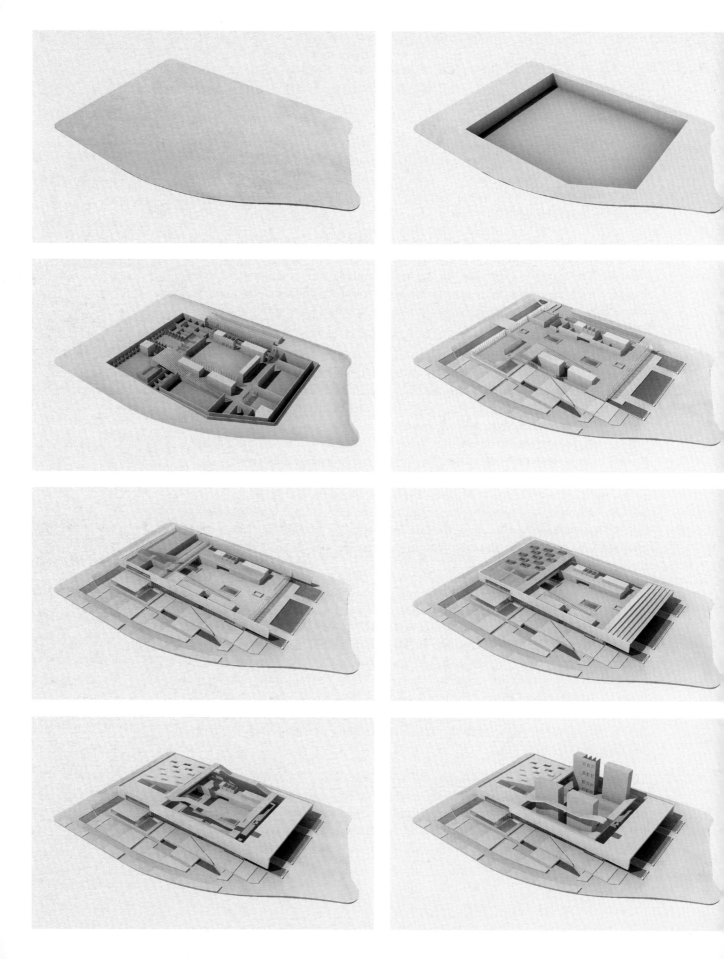

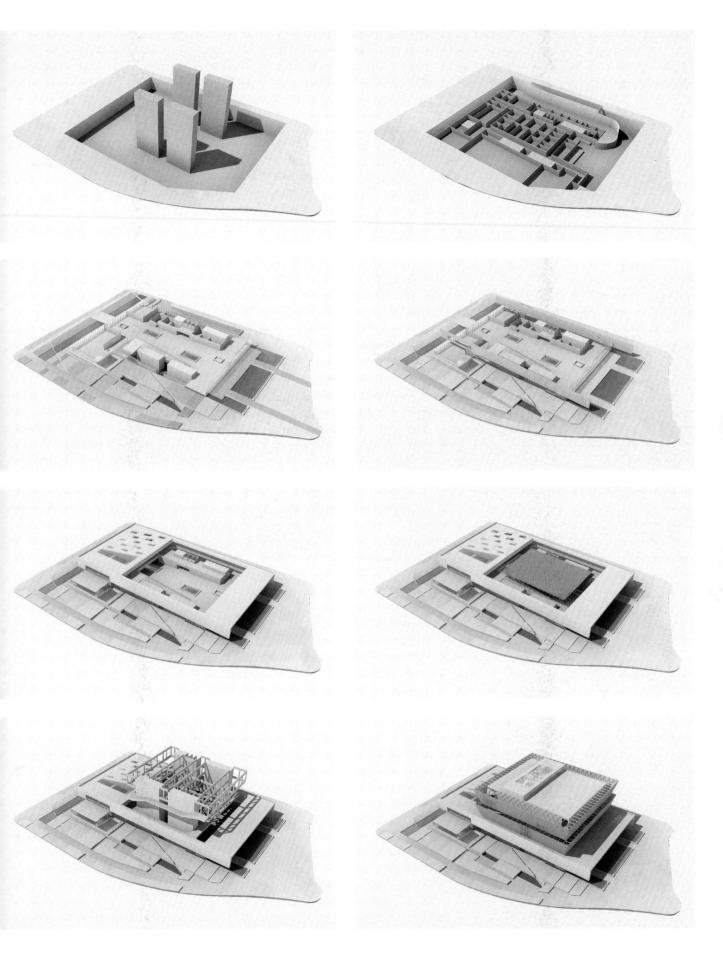

hired a lead team of highly experienced construction companies: Clark Construction Group, Smoot Construction, and H. J. Russell & Company. This new joint venture included minority-owned construction firms and supported local businesses—both of which were project goals—and was to be responsible for the Museum's construction over a period of several years.

To coordinate this process, both the design and construction teams used innovative building information–modeling software that allowed the architects, engineers, and contractors to work collaboratively on a virtual model of the Museum. To support the structure, the architects and engineers designed a large truss system supported by four large concrete service cores. The trusses support the load of the upper-level galleries and permit open gallery spaces that are free from columns. The Corona's armature and the glass curtain wall attach to a steel truss frame connected at the top to the fifth-level slab and also at ground level. As an independent sheath wrapping the building, the three tiers of the Corona do not align at any point with the Museum's four upper levels. All of the architectural spaces, structural components, material choices, and mechanical systems, such as plumbing, heating and cooling, were layered into the virtual model to allow for the coordination of trades and the real-time management of cost and efficiencies.

Previous pages: Early computer-generated diagrams showing how the Museum's spaces, structural elements (including its grand Porch), and façade fit together onsite, 2009.

Opposite: Evolution of the Museum's design, from a two-tiered Corona (*top*) to the final three-tiered version (*bottom*).

BREAKING NEW GROUND

On February 22, 2012, a mild winter morning, President Barack Obama led the momentous groundbreaking ceremony for the National Museum of African American History and Culture.

Fittingly, the site chosen for the Museum lies on a symbolic axis that connects to the U.S. Capitol and the White House. The public joined the Smithsonian's leadership and staff, local and national political leaders, Museum Council members, corporate sponsors, individual donors, and the architectural and construction teams in celebrating this auspicious moment in American history.

President Obama gave a stirring speech emphasizing why the National Mall is the appropriate home for a museum of black history and culture. He reminded the audience that it was here that "the pillars of democracy were built, often by black hands. And it is on this spot—alongside the monuments to those who gave birth to this nation, and those who worked so hard to perfect it—that generations will remember the sometimes difficult, often inspirational, but always central role that African Americans have played in the life of our country. This museum will celebrate that history."

Representative John Lewis, who had cosponsored the legislation that made the initiative a reality, observed on that joyous morning: "What we witnessed today will go down in history.... It is the substance of things hoped for and the validation of our dreams."

Director Bunch conveyed the importance of a museum that takes a radical stance toward the country's history and its lessons, stating that "there are few things as powerful as a people, a nation steeped in its history, and there is nothing nobler than honoring all our ancestors by remembering the full, rich, and diverse history of America."

Top: President Barack Obama (with Founding Director Lonnie G. Bunch III) speaking at the Museum groundbreaking ceremony, February 2012. *Bottom:* Groundbreaking attendees include (*left to right*) Richard Parsons, Patty Stonesifer, former First Lady Laura Bush, Secretary of the Smithsonian G. Wayne Clough, Director Lonnie G. Bunch III, Richard Kurin, France Córdova, and Linda Johnson Rice.

PART 2

Memory of Place

CHAPTER 5
CRAFTING MEMORY &
MEANING

With its eye-catching Corona and Porch, its galleries filled with innovative exhibitions on the history, culture, and communities of black Americans, and its distinctive landscaping celebrating the African American journey, the architecture of the National Museum of African American History and Culture introduces a different kind of museum to the nation's public commons, the National Mall.

Lead designer David Adjaye wanted to create a "spectacular and amazing building." Inspired by the Museum's charge to tell a different American story, he and the design team imagined an unparalleled structure that would make "people's jaws drop because it's a new kind of building and a new kind of museum." The Smithsonian team, led by Director Lonnie Bunch and FAB/S, agreed that the design had to draw upon, in the words of Adjaye, "narratives that were emotionally important." The architecture needed to engage visitors about histories that defy easy explanations.

View of the National Museum of African American History and Culture, looking across the north lawn and the busy thoroughfare of 14th Street NW.

One way to make stories meaningful and memorable is to tie them to spaces that people can recognize. When people create places and inhabit them, whether they are houses or parks, churches or neighborhoods, these locales express their shared aspirations. When a person leaves a place, it often stays imprinted in his or her memory and the shared memory of others. In her book *Beloved*, novelist Toni Morrison captured the poignancy of place in an observation: "If a house burns down, it's gone, but the place—the picture of it—stays, and not just in my rememory, but out there, in the world."

African Americans brought memories of place from parts of Africa to different regions of the New World. As is the nature of all recollection, the chaff was forgotten, revealing more clearly the treasured kernel of the memory. The various journeys of black Americans—forced and voluntary—dispersed these sensibilities to all corners of the United States, where they became part of the American landscape.

The South's "hush" or "brush harbors" (secret meeting places during slavery) and shotgun houses, Yoruban architectural columns, and antebellum cast-iron grillwork all inspired the unique design of the National Museum of African American History and Culture. For more than three hundred years, these unique sites and architectural features served as places and visual reminders of spaces where African Americans shared the bonds of family, community, and citizenship. In recalling these places, some of them little known or forgotten, the architecture and design support the Museum's mission to "bridge a gap in our national memory."

The FAB/S team approached the Museum not just as a building, but also as a landscape. The forest became a central motif for lead designer Adjaye, one that he used to enhance both the building and its setting. The forest speaks to the history of African American craft, construction, and spirituality, and it also connects African Americans to their roots in the forested regions of West Africa. When enslaved Africans arrived in the Americas, their memories of home influenced their practices of building and farming. For instance, the early construction of the wooden two-room "ti-kay" cottage in the Caribbean was carried forward in the American shotgun house. For Adjaye, the design of the Museum, amid the impressive but reserved buildings of Washington, D.C., offered a way in which the "black scenography of architectural space can play a counter to the classical, traditional way of making space and offer really creative alternatives."

FAB/S imagined the Museum as an ensemble of dense forest and clearings, an interplay of shelter and spaces for gatherings. The basic form of the building, a series of nested gallery and public spaces that visitors traverse threshold by threshold, mirrors the unfolding story of black American culture and history.

The FAB/S design uses the visual and tactile character of materials—water, bronze, and wood—to evoke specific histories of craft and construction in the African Diaspora. Water is an important symbolic element in both the landscaping and the building's interior. Bronze influences the color and material of the regal Corona. Wood, the material of the forest, can be found in parts of the interior. The materials selected for the floors, walls, and ceilings directly engage the visitor's senses, allowing sight, sound, smell, and touch to directly influence the memory of place. The color and texture of materials can make a large, monumental building feel more intimate and personal.

A central example of a place of memory that influenced the Museum's design is the hush or brush harbor of the American South. Even though slavery limited their movement, freed and enslaved blacks in the 1700s and 1800s created secret places of worship as well as resistance. Enslaved Africans often created these community places in the woods at the edges of plantations or on the banks of a river or stream, because water symbolized renewal in their religious ceremonies. Men and women would clear the area by cutting back the trees and shrubs and use rocks and logs for seating. Groups used the clearing not only for worship, but also for funeral services and celebrations. Enslaved Africans would quietly steal away from the plantation to their hush harbors in the forest, far from the watchful eyes of the overseers and masters. In many areas of the South, such gatherings, particularly religious ones, were illegal because slave owners feared participants would plot a rebellion or riot. Such fears were not unfounded. In 1822, freed former slave Denmark Vesey, inspired by the ideals of liberty that had sparked the American Revolution and Haitian Revolution, met his co-conspirators in the woods surrounding Charleston to plan a revolt against slaveholders. The fear of insurrection led to the passage of laws that banned both free and enslaved African Americans from convening religious services unless a white minister presided.

Nevertheless, beneath the cloak of the night sky in the antebellum South, men, women, and children would gather under the trees. During their religious services, they would raise their voices in song, which would echo into the outstretched branches of the natural enclosure. Their passionate singing of spirituals expressed a yearning to escape from a life of ceaseless toil in the plantation fields or the master's household, from the constant threat of beatings or rape, and from the fear that a family member might be sold. These poignant songs reflected a profound desire to experience freedom in the United States, a young nation founded on the principles of democracy.

A Plantation Burial (1860), by John Antrobus. Enslaved men and women gather for a burial in a clearing much like the hush or brush harbors used for secret meetings and worship.

Prayer formed an important part of these religious services. Over the course of the sermon, the preacher's voice would rise in volume and intensity. As the sermon's cadence quickened, the preacher would call out to the congregation, who would respond with greater intensity. Moved by the spiritual exchange, men and women would stand up and raise their hands in jubilation. The preacher's uplifting sermon would inspire some of the congregation to sing and dance by stomping on the ground as they moved in a circle, while the rest of the congregation clapped their hands to mark the rhythm of the dance. This spirited dance was called a ring shout. The angled profile of the Corona that sheathes the Museum symbolizes the joyful gesture of arms raised in praise and celebration.

But the reference to the ring shout also alludes to a time and place predating the Atlantic slave trade. Enslaved Africans carried memories of West African ring ceremonies (held to pay homage to ancestors) with them on the Middle Passage to the Americas. Their African beliefs merged with European and Christian traditions in a process called creolization or hybridization, the mixing of cultures so characteristic of the U.S. melting pot. In this way, the Corona also symbolizes the worldwide African Diaspora.

With such a rich heritage to draw upon, the architects found a wide variety of elements that would allow the building itself to tell the African American story.

Left to right: The architecture's rich African American and African symbolic language: a carved Yoruban caryatid, which influenced the stepped pyramidal shape of the Corona; hands raised in jubilation, reflected in the tiers' upward motion; a southern porch, the basis for the Museum's own welcoming Porch; and agricultural furrows, which inspired the grass-and-stone bands of the Reading Grove.

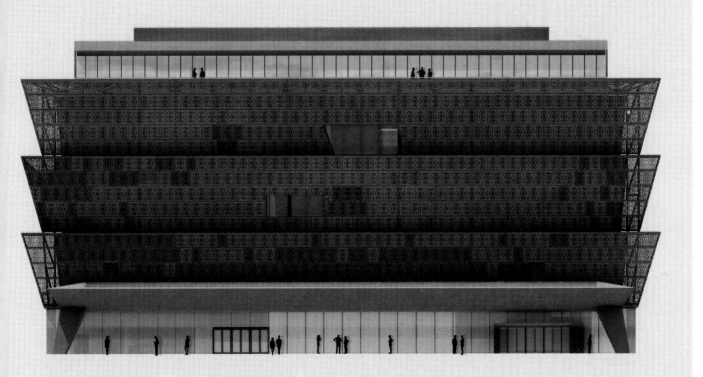

The Corona

To design the Corona, Adjaye, Freelon, and the FAB/S team gathered narratives from African and African American experiences of place making. The shimmering bronze façade represents the difficult journey the country has taken to fulfill its ideals of liberty for all Americans. When illuminated at night, the delicate screen panels appear to hover above the ground like a lantern.

Its lattice pattern and structure, the outcome of a long FAB/S dialogue with Director Bunch, hold a wealth of symbolism. The different techniques and forms used in its construction, for example, reflect the complex cultural exchanges that occurred between the kingdoms and territories of West Africa and the Americas and Caribbean.

National Museum of African American History and Culture, illuminated at night.

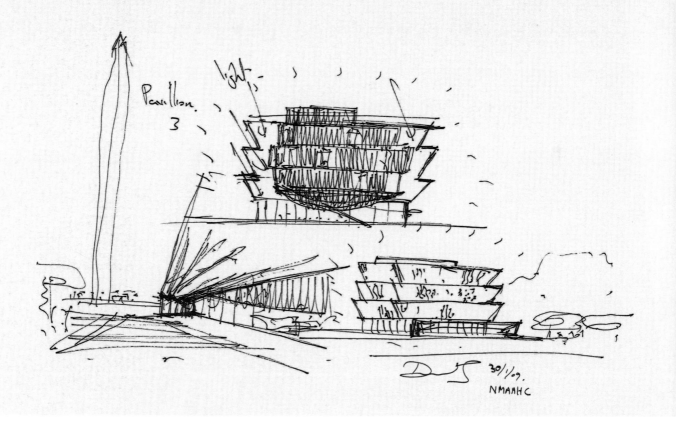

Pavillion.
3

30/1/09.
NMAAHC

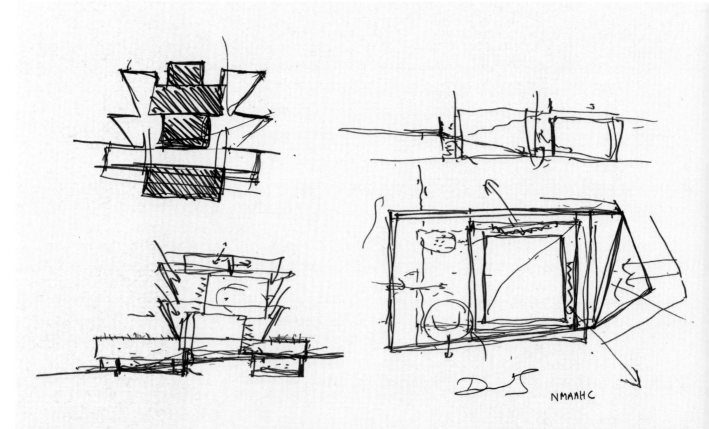

NMAAHC

Inspiration also came from the West African caryatid—a column in human or animal form that supported the verandas of major religious shrines in Yorubaland, in what is now Nigeria. Caryatids lined a king's ceremonial courtyard to form a sacred space of worship. Carved from wood by expert sculptors such as the Yoruban artist Olowe of Ise, who worked in the early 1900s, such caryatids represented noble male, female, and animal figures. They honored the kingdom's sacred divinities and symbolized its social hierarchy. Using wood, Olowe of Ise carved one-, two- and three-tiered inverted pyramid forms, the equivalent of a classical column capital, to bridge the heads of caryatid figures and the structural crossbeam of the veranda.

However, Adjaye was not interested in finding direct models from a particular building or work of art, because he wanted to avoid specifically European, American, African American, or African motifs. Instead, he sought forms that "linked the architecture, geography, and people of Africa and African America—the veranda and the porch." Inspired by their elegance and significance in West African architecture, Adjaye abstracted the top of the caryatids and their angled sides as a reference for the three-stacked tiers of the Corona. His early sketches show how two ideas—the caryatid and the praise gesture of raised arms, practiced in the hush harbors—merged into the Corona's angular form.

The Corona also reflects its surroundings on the National Mall and its relation to the Washington Monument, designed by Robert Mills in 1845 and modeled on an Egyptian obelisk. The Corona's seventeen-degree angle matches that of the pyramidal capstone of the Washington Monument, and the size and placement of the Corona's panels draw inspiration from the arrangement of the obelisk's stones, the "bond pattern" that makes it strong. The reference to the Washington Monument also highlights the historical influence of the African architecture of Nubia and Egypt on ancient Greek and Roman architecture. This in turn inspired the neoclassical and Beaux-Arts style of many of the buildings in Washington, D.C., including the White House, the Capitol Building, and the National Gallery of Art's West Wing.

Opposite, top: Early conceptual sketch of the Museum's Porch canopy in relation to the Washington Monument (2009), by design architect David Adjaye. Also noted is the filtration of sunlight through the Corona and into the public spaces. *Opposite, bottom:* Adjaye's sketches of the upper and lower galleries nested inside the Corona (*left*) and the circulation of visitors into and around the Museum (*right*), 2009.

Right: Three-tiered wooden caryatid carved by Yoruban artist Olowe of Ise, ca. 1900.

The wrought- and cast-iron screens crafted by enslaved and freed African American blacksmiths on the porches, balconies, and gates of Charleston, New Orleans, and other parts of the American South were another inspiration. Although unrecognized for this work—historians took little note of these craftsmen's talents—black American ironworkers gave these port cities their distinctive character. Such artistry, as Director Bunch has observed, is often hiding in plain sight in cities and towns across the country. Metalworking was a prized skill with ancient roots in Africa. The knowledge of ironworking spread through West Africa starting around 600 BCE and flourished in the Dahomey, Benin, and Yoruba kingdoms, where bronze and other metals had spiritual resonance.

Philip Simmons (1992), who crafted more than five hundred gates, screens, and grilles in and around Charleston, South Carolina.

In America, slaveholders were quick to utilize the knowledge of enslaved men from these kingdoms, hiring out their workers to large foundries. Some slaveholders permitted their men to earn and save money to buy their families' freedom. In addition, numerous freed ironworkers set up their own workshops. At one point, Charleston had almost as many black ironworkers as white. The basic styles and patterns were European and Spanish, but black artisans also introduced their own expressive forms, including symbols derived from particular African cultures. Adinkra, Sankofa, and symbols from other African kingdoms, for example, feature in the ironwork of New Orleans. Historical accounts of the architecture rarely identify the craftsmen. For seven decades, master blacksmith Philip Simmons crafted more than five hundred gates, screens, and grilles in Charleston, yet his artistry wasn't publicly recognized until the 1980s. The Museum honors the creativity and labor of these artists.

In studying the form, function, and material of cast-iron grilles, FAB/S made another discovery that influenced the Corona's signature panels. African American ironworkers in the South constructed grilles by casting hot liquid iron in sand molds. They then welded the pieces together into distinctive arabesques in a manner Adjaye likened to the way architects draft: line by line. The design team analyzed an antique grille gate from Charleston to understand how its geometry was organized, studying how its cast-iron leaves were welded together to create the structure that held all the pieces together.

Opposite: Eighteenth- and nineteenth-century African American ironwork from Charleston and New Orleans, used to develop the pattern of the Corona panels. *Top row:* The design team first abstracted ornamentation from historical grilles into mirrored and repeated patterns. *Middle and bottom rows:* The patterns' opacity was then staggered at various percentages to achieve optimum heat gain and cooling for the Museum building.

Historic Precedents: New Orleans Balconies

Charleston Gates-
Nodes/Weld

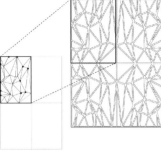

Triangulate

Pattern

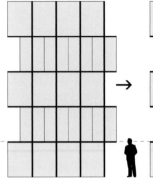
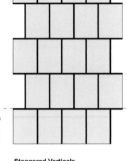

Vertical / Horizontal
Most efficient, but least attractive from interior

Vertical runs through the middle of the panel

Staggered Verticals
Aligns to panel edges

Structurally difficult due to indirect load path
between top and bottom of corona tier

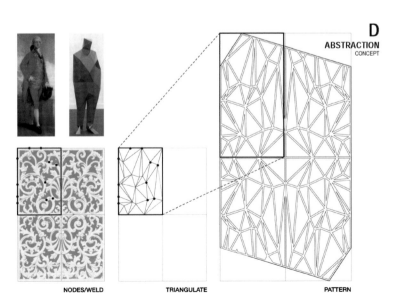

NODES/WELD

TRIANGULATE

PATTERN

D
ABSTRACTION
CONCEPT

75%

70%

65%

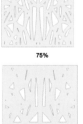
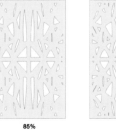

90%

85%

80%

PANEL GRADATION
(PERCENTAGE OF OPACITY)

Based on this observation, the architects drew a diagram that abstracted the weld points into nodes, revealing that the geometric pattern of the screen was composed of four panels that were mirrored and then flipped. FAB/S adapted this abstract pattern as the basis of the design for the panels of the Corona.

On balconies and porches in the South, the lattice structure of the ornamental iron grilles has long provided welcome relief from intense summer heat and humidity. FAB/S updated this function with an innovative system that changes the opacity of the Corona's panels. Using parametric design software, Adjaye and the architectural team were able to experiment with the size of the openings and the thickness of the metal members. The openings are calibrated at 65, 75, 85, and 90 percent density. The variation in the openings allows the panels, each measuring three by five feet, to achieve optimum heat gain and cooling, an important consideration in the hot summers of Washington, D.C. The variety of panel densities

Coated cast-aluminum Corona panels being attached to the Museum's structural frame, 2015.

reduces direct sunlight heat gains and boosts the energy efficiency of the building by reducing the heating and cooling loads on the mechanical systems, a major component of the Museum's green credentials. The panels' design also allowed the architects to vary the amount of natural light according to the needs of the interior spaces.

FAB/S and the design-assist team provided by the construction team worked with structural engineer Guy Nordenson to design an exterior frame of horizontal and vertical trusses connecting the fifth level of the Museum and the concrete slab at ground level. The Corona panels were then placed in a vertical pattern and attached to the steel

Southeast corner of the Museum, along 14th Street NW, 2015. The Corona's exterior frame connects the fifth level to the ground-level concrete foundation.

truss frame surrounding the Museum's glass curtain wall. Holding carefully placed counterweights, this armature balanced the load of the individual Corona panels as construction workers attached the panels to the supporting frame. This inventive structural solution allows the Corona to apparently float.

At the beginning of the design process, Adjaye, Freelon, and the design team envisioned cast-bronze panels for the Corona, but their weight would have been too great to support without increasing the depth of the structural members and exceeding the allowed height. After several rounds of testing materials for color and weight, the final selection, coated cast aluminum, achieved a visual feel similar to bronze while being much lighter. At the same time, the composite provided the durability, cost benefits, and maintenance efficiencies necessary for a museum that will be around for many years. Before leaving the factory, the panels were coated with a durable powder-coat finish containing metallic elements that reflect a range of luminescent colors: red-bronze, copper, and dark brown,

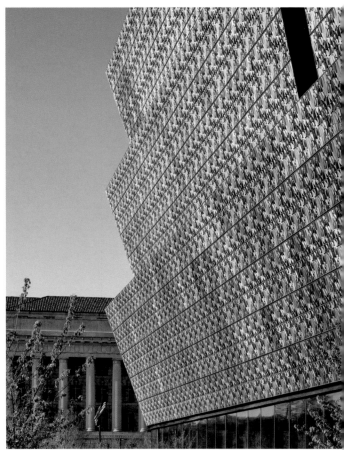
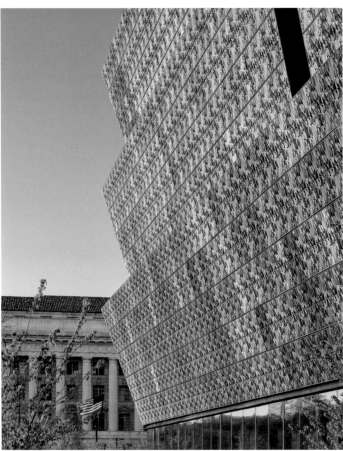

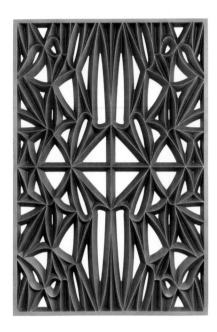

Close-up of a Corona panel. Its intricate sculptural details reflect sunlight in many directions.

with hints of brass and dark gold. The panels required rigorous material testing and review in order to obtain the correct balance of color, reflection, and texture. A team of architects, engineers, contractors, Smithsonian staff, and members of the Commission of Fine Arts visited a full-scale mockup of a section of the Corona at the factory in Pennsylvania to approve the progress of its design and development.

Because the coated cast-aluminum panels have a sculpted, V-shaped profile, sunlight reflects off the screens in different ways, creating a three-dimensional effect of light and shadow depending on the time of day and the angle at which the viewer sees the Corona. The façade may look different from Constitution Avenue than from the Washington Monument. By choosing sculpted panels, the architects ensured that the façade radiates a soft golden color under a noontime sun.

Viewing the building in the late afternoon, by contrast, reveals deep bronze colors on one side that mellow to a pinkish glow at the other end. On a cloudy day, the screen flattens to a burnished sepia hue. Derek Ross, the Smithsonian's engineer, admires how the light plays with the façade both inside and outside: "In the morning, the light has a different dynamic—it shimmers. In the middle of the day, it flattens out so the surfaces are not shiny, but in the evening the light starts to dance again as the sunlight casts shadows of the Corona onto the interior walls." At night, the illuminated Corona glows like the bonfires that guided enslaved men, women, and children to freedom along the Underground Railroad. In all, the architects designed the Corona's variegated hues to capture the many moods that the African American story evokes.

Opposite: Varying hues of the Corona in shifting sunlight (*left to right, top to bottom*): early morning, midmorning, afternoon, and evening.

Following pages: Night vista of the National Museum of African American History and Culture, seen from the Washington Monument Grounds. In the distance is the U.S. Capitol.

LANDSCAPES OF MEMORY

The Museum's architects have incorporated moving experiences into the exterior spaces. The alternating horizontal bands of grass and stone in the Reading Grove evoke agricultural furrows receding into the horizon, while the colorful flowers and foliage—pale pink, bright yellow, deep red, and dark green—pay homage to the vibrant hues of the multicolored bottle trees that enliven the yards of African Americans in the rural South.

Kathryn Gustafson, of landscape architectural firm Gustafson Guthrie Nichol, worked closely with FAB/S and the Smithsonian's team of landscape architects to finalize the design of the five-acre site. Gustafson's designs burst with color and contrasting textures to evoke various black American places of memory. Working with sketches and clay models, she crafted a series of unique experiences that convey both the African American spiritual connection to the land and different features of the American landscape.

Thousands of crocuses blooming in spring on the Museum's north lawn, recalling the glass beads that African Americans used in charms and amulets to symbolize hospitality in the eighteenth and nineteenth centuries.

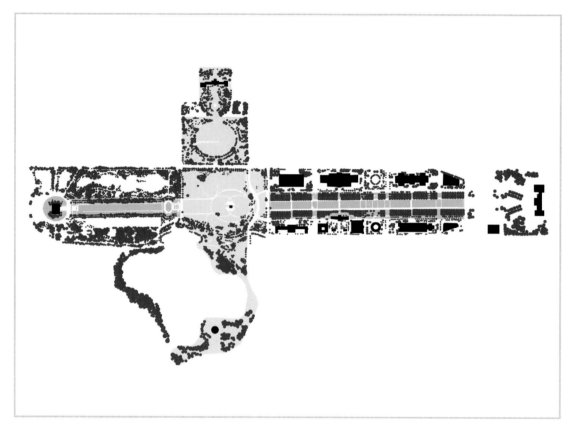

Figure-ground diagram depicting the National Mall's buildings (colored black) in relation to its landscape (green). It shows that the Museum's site forms a hinge between the east-west axis from the U.S. Capitol to the Lincoln Memorial and the north-south axis between the Washington Monument and the White House.

The gardens form part of a wider landscape overseen by Smithsonian Gardens, which manages 180 acres of grounds around the Smithsonian's facilities in Washington, D.C. Many of the gardens function as outdoor museums, where visitors can explore different styles of garden design and discover a diverse array of plants, trees, shrubs, and flowers. The gardens educate the public about how plant and animal diversity contribute to healthy ecosystems.

Africans arrived in the Americas with a deep knowledge of farming and animal husbandry gleaned from the forests and savannas of their homeland. Their work in the rice, tobacco, and cotton fields during slavery and the post-emancipation period fueled the economic prosperity that elevated the United States to a world power. The African American relationship to the vast and varied terrain of the United States has parallels with the wider American experience of a land that has sustained and nurtured its people. However, the exploitation of a people trapped first in slavery and then in sharecropping yields other, more traumatic stories that are, for Director Bunch, "the difficult, the controversial, and the defeats" that are also part of American history.

While the National Museum of African American History and Culture has its unique attractions, it also continues the tradition of other museums on the National Mall; it, too, is a repository of the nation's history. The Mall began to take shape in 1791, when President George Washington selected French engineer Pierre Charles L'Enfant to plan a capital city on the banks of the Potomac River. He made his first drawings from a survey of the marshy hundred-square-mile tract, which included calculations made by a free African American surveyor named Benjamin Banneker. From those drawings, L'Enfant laid out the plans for the Federal City, as Washington was originally called. The core of the city was a grand avenue, four hundred feet wide. This central band of open park space was planted with trees and lined on both sides with neoclassical buildings and monuments. It became the National Mall.

Washington, D.C., was founded on land donated from two slaveholding states: Maryland and Virginia. The labor of enslaved men, women, and children contributed to the everyday life of the new city. Enslaved Africans constructed many of the civic buildings and most likely excavated the original trench for the Tiber Creek canal that once ran along the northern edge of the Mall. As the city grew, brick manufacturers hired enslaved men from their masters.

The wider Chesapeake region also maintained a lucrative slave trade network. As a New York abolitionist broadside from the 1830s documents, Washington, D.C., had its share of slave pens, auction houses, and slave jails, including some just beyond the National Mall. The city's slave traders routinely marched slave coffles—groups of chained men, women, and children—past the U.S. Capitol on their way to southern markets. Slavery was an integral part of the city's early economy. These are the difficult truths that the Museum building and its exhibitions seek to show.

By 1902, the L'Enfant scheme had not been fully realized, and the McMillan Commission revived its visionary design. This federal panel of leading architects, including Daniel Burnham, Charles F. McKim, and landscape architect Frederick Law Olmsted Jr., as well as artist Augustus Saint-Gaudens, were entrusted with redesigning the National Mall. They planned grand rows of trees and wide lawns and aligned the Beaux-Arts façades of the Mall's civic buildings to give the central site a more cohesive character.

The parcel of land on which the Museum stands forms a hinge between the orthogonal axis of the National Mall conceived by L'Enfant's original plan and the picturesque north-south axis that extends from the White House to the Jefferson Memorial, intersecting at the Washington Monument Grounds. The landscape takes advantage of these two contrasting geometries. On the north side of the Museum, Gustafson and her team designed the paths to mimic the preexisting curved walkways leading to the Washington Monument and the nearby White House Ellipse.

The landscape design also had to mediate between the urban character of Constitution Avenue to the north and the open park space on the south side. On the north side,

A wall of polished granite on the approach toward the Museum from Constitution Avenue mirroring the sky.

an allée (alley) of American elm trees lines both sides of the sidewalk, as is typical on Constitution Avenue, and complements the landscape design of the adjacent National Museum of American History. The walkway to the National Museum of African American History and Culture gradually slopes up from the street so that, uniquely for the museums on the Mall, all visitors enter the Museum on the same level and begin their journey together.

Gustafson and her team designed a long wall of highly polished black granite to define the threshold of the Museum's grounds. The wall's seventeen-degree angle matches that of the Corona and the Washington Monument's capstone and ties together the key places of memory that form the grounds' narrative. The granite mirrors the sky and the clouds to create a water-like reflection. In addition, this long, curved wall of reflected blue evokes the historical Tiber Creek, whose waters once flowed through the site.

Opposite, top: A row of patriot elms along the 14th Street NW side of the Museum offers shade in summer. *Bottom:* View from the Porch looking across the Museum's expansive fountain to the National Mall. Built of black granite and inscribed with quotes from abolitionist Frederick Douglass and writer James Baldwin, the fountain's flowing and still waters suggest the arduous African American journey toward full rights of citizenship.

Plaza around the Oculus, which filters light into the Museum's Contemplative Court, located belowground.

A walkway cuts through the wall to form a bridge that recalls the difficult journey of the Middle Passage.

Gustafson and her team selected a variety of plant colors and textures to create a changing panorama around the Museum. Every spring, the north lawn becomes a vast blue carpet of 390,000 crocuses. This sea of blue, resembling rushing water as it ripples in the spring breezes, also references the blue beads in charms and amulets used by African Americans to symbolize hospitality in the eighteenth and nineteenth centuries.

Throughout the exterior and interior spaces, Gustafson Guthrie Nichol and FAB/S employ the powerful symbolism of water as a medium of healing and renewal in African American cultural practices. In song, literature, art, and poetry, rivers and oceans traditionally represent a means of escape from bondage and deliverance to the Promised Land. Langston Hughes's poem "The Negro Speaks of Rivers" eloquently captures the deep spiritual and historical relationship that African Americans have to water, from the rivers of the Congo and the Nile to the Mississippi, in its closing line: "My soul has grown deep like the rivers."

Opposite: Black granite benches in the Reading Grove, arranged in interlocking U shapes to represent the mutually reinforcing beliefs of hope and optimism.

Two walkways on the grounds lead to a plaza around the Oculus, whose clerestory windows filter light into the Contemplative Court inside the Museum. Benches provide a place for visitors to rest and admire the exterior of the Museum before proceeding to the north entrance or to the south side and the Washington Monument. At night, the Oculus illuminates the grounds. The circular beacon recalls the church steeples and the lanterns in safe houses along Underground Railroad, by which enslaved people fled to freedom.

The nearby Reading Grove is dedicated to hope and optimism. Groups can gather in the Reading Grove to listen to Museum docents give talks about the plants and trees or to hear about the black history of Washington, D.C. The black granite benches are arranged in two interlocking U shapes, representing the mutually reinforcing beliefs of hope and optimism that propelled black Americans along their journey toward equality and justice. The landscape architects selected American elm trees and purple-leafed copper beech trees to surround the Reading Grove, with live oaks near the Oculus in honor of the majestic Emancipation Oak at Hampton University in Virginia, where, in 1863, the Emancipation Proclamation was first read to black Americans in the South.

Visitors catch some of the most impressive views of the Corona, framed by colorful trees and flowers, from the National Mall on the south side. Different types of American elms ring the entire Museum, emblematic of the original thousand elms planted in the 1930s along the National Mall's length. The landscape architects chose the contrasting colors of katsura trees, whose leaves change from blue-green to reddish purple, and ginkgo trees, whose leaves turn from green to bright yellow, for the South Plaza. Aromatic sassafras trees, whose leaves are used for medicinal purposes by Native Americans and ground into spices in Creole cooking, are also planted here. Once fully mature, the elms, beeches, and other trees will provide ample shade for pedestrians and the Museum. The trees also allude to the hush harbors, where slaves met in secret.

Several different types of understory trees, such as Japanese flowering cherry trees, white fringe, and magnolia trees, are planted throughout the grounds. Gustafson and her team selected two types of cherry trees to link the Museum site to the storied cherry trees that line the Tidal Basin and those around the Washington Monument. The flowers of the Museum's dogwood trees offer an additional burst of color in spring. This array of trees creates a rich vista of blossoms, leaf colors, and textures that enlivens the Museum grounds year-round.

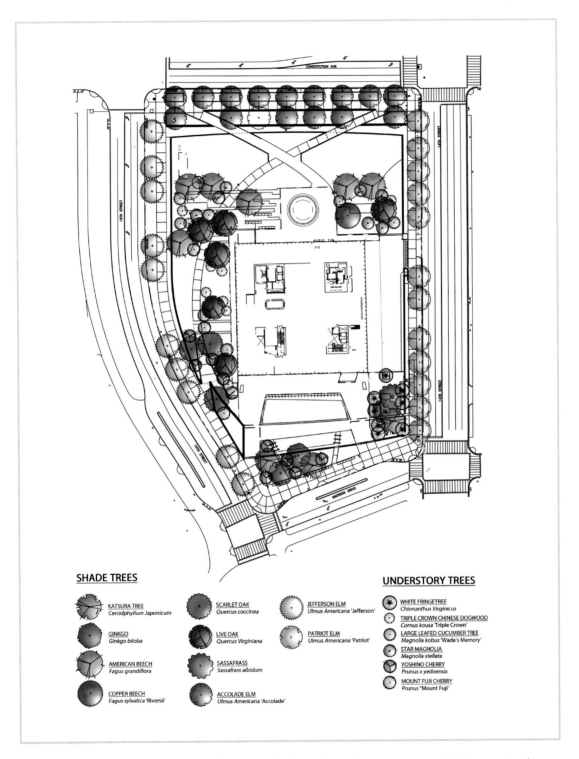

SHADE TREES

KATSURA TREE *Cercidphyllum Japonicum*	**SCARLET OAK** *Quercus coccinea*	**JEFFERSON ELM** *Ulmus Americana 'Jefferson'*
GINKGO *Ginkgo biloba*	**LIVE OAK** *Quercus Virginiana*	**PATRIOT ELM** *Ulmus Americana 'Patriot'*
AMERICAN BEECH *Fagus grandiflora*	**SASSAFRASS** *Sassafrass albidum*	
COPPER BEECH *Fagus sylvatica 'Riversii'*	**ACCOLADE ELM** *Ulmus Americana 'Accolade'*	

UNDERSTORY TREES

WHITE FRINGETREE *Chionanthus Virginicus*	
TRIPLE CROWN CHINESE DOGWOOD *Cornus kousa 'Triple Crown'*	
LARGE LEAFED CUCUMBER TREE *Magnolia kobus 'Wada's Memory'*	
STAR MAGNOLIA *Magnolia stellata*	
YOSHINO CHERRY *Prunus x yedoensis*	
MOUNT FUJI CHERRY *Prunus "Mount Fuji'*	

Katsura, gingko, elm, oak, cherry, beech, sassafras, magnolia, dogwood, and other tree species on the Museum grounds, surrounding the building with colors and textures that change with the seasons.

A WELCOMING PORCH

A porch, a covered outdoor space, is an integral part of the shotgun house, a one-room-wide cottage with a pitched roof that is found all over the South. The small house derives its nickname from the legend that a bullet fired from a gun at the front door would travel straight through the house and out the back door. Because its rooms are arranged in a linear fashion, the house makes efficient and economical use of building materials, typically wood.

The compact organization of the shotgun house has other advantages. In some areas, builders erected shotgun houses with tall ceilings and opposing openings so that when residents opened the windows in the front and back, a cool breeze was drawn through the house. This efficient channeling of air kept the structure well ventilated during the hot summer months. The Museum's architects used a similar strategy of sustainable design to create the microclimate of the Porch, a striking feature of the main entrance, facing onto the National Mall. Here a breeze, cooled as it moves over the water of the adjacent pool, replaces hot air below the Porch.

Some scholars believe that the design of the linear cottage derives from that of small two-room dwellings constructed in parts of West Africa, including today's Senegal,

Previous pages: The National Museum of African American History and Culture (*left, center*) seen in relation to the White House and the Washington Monument. *Opposite:* The Porch and its cantilevered canopy, which extend the entire length of the Museum's south façade along the National Mall.

African Americans on the porches of shotgun houses in Georgia, ca.1900.

Guinea-Bissau, and Gambia. Beginning in the 1500s, enslaved Africans brought to work in the sugarcane fields on Caribbean plantations adapted the West African house to suit the local climate, building materials, and construction techniques. In Haiti, this type of two-room house was called a ti-kay. In Haiti's villages and towns, Europeans and free people of color, who also owned enslaved Africans, built larger versions of the linear cottage, whose form was well suited to the tropical climate.

The idea migrated to the United States in the 1790s, when many white French, free people of color, and African slaves fled Haiti to escape the social unrest stirred up by Toussaint Louverture and ending with the Haitian Revolution, which freed the colony's slaves. The fleeing refugees settled in what was the French colony of Louisiana before it was purchased by the United States in 1803.

Free and enslaved builders arriving in New Orleans brought their knowledge of linear cottage construction. By the 1830s, the shotgun house could be found in many neighborhoods of the city. As people migrated up and down the Mississippi River and along other routes, place memory traveled with them. Shotgun houses were built in rural areas and cities across Mississippi, Texas, the Carolinas, Alabama, Tennessee, and Kentucky. In the early 1800s, builders attached a porch. The roof extension provided shade for the inhabitants, especially on hot summer days, and could be used for storage and for work. The deep overhang also cooled the house by preventing scorching sunrays from penetrating the front of the house.

Man shucking ears of corn on a porch, 1938. As an extension of interior living areas, southern porches were spaces for both domestic activities and public life.

Porches formed dynamic social spaces that linked the domestic realm inside the house to the bustling street life or farm activities outside it. Residents and visitors used the outdoor area for all kinds of activities: Women would snap green beans while watching the children play; elders would sit and rest there or tell stories. Protected from the elements, porches served as spaces for sorting and storing wood, sweet potatoes, cotton, and other crops on their way to market. In her novel *Their Eyes Were Watching God*, which takes place in the black town of Eatonville, Florida, Zora Neale Hurston captured the vitality of porch life: "Jody was on the porch and the porch was full of Eatonville." Residents placed seats, typically rocking chairs, on the porch or hung swings specifically designed for the outdoor space. These provided prime seats to watch the panorama of daily life unfold. The porch was where people learned about local news and events happening around the country. This spirit of porch life inspired Adjaye, Freelon, and the FAB/S team to design a porch for the Museum, one that projects that same gesture of hospitality to everyone passing the building along the National Mall.

In the post–Civil War era, owning a home was, for many black families, a social symbol of upward mobility. The appearance conveyed by the front porch—its tidy furniture and neat pots of flowers—became an indication of respectability. As black Americans moved northward with the Great Migration from the 1910s through the 1950s, the sensibilities of place making traveled with them. The social life of the porch was transferred to the urban stoop.

The Museum's Porch is large enough to welcome visitors from all over the world. The spectacular overhang spans the entire length of the building, shading the South Plaza's

The Museum's Porch, welcoming visitors in the summer, when the combination of water and shade creates a cool and comfortable microclimate on the South Plaza.

open terrace. It forms a threshold between the Museum's exterior and the central Heritage Hall inside. Here the southern porch meets its cousin, the West African veranda. The Porch also echoes the National Mall's ensemble of public spaces, which include the portico entry of the National Museum of Natural History, the terrace of the National Museum of American History, and the sculpture garden of the National Gallery of Art.

The monumental scale of the Porch required a carefully engineered design solution by engineers Guy Nordenson and Associates. The Porch's overhang, a full two hundred feet long, extends forty-four feet from the Corona and tapers to a six-inch edge. The large steel truss columns at either end are engineered to carry the load of the trusses that span its length. Tilted up at an angle, the Porch's underside, in a light-gray hue, captures the shimmering light reflecting off the South Plaza's pool, giving people a visually charged moment when entering the Museum.

Before the public enters the Museum from the south, they pass a dramatic black granite fountain, a collaborative design by Gustafson Guthrie Nichol and FAB/S. Its themes of moving and still water symbolize the difficult history of African Americans in their quest for full rights of citizenship. To promote the Museum's core message of understanding and reconciliation, Director Bunch selected verses from nineteenth-century abolitionist Frederick Douglass and twentieth-century writer James Baldwin to inscribe on its stones.

The quote from Douglass calls attention to the basic human origins of freedom:

> *Liberty exists in the very idea of man's creation. It was his even before he comprehended it. He was created in it, endowed with it, and it can never be taken away.*

Baldwin's quote is a reminder of the vital importance of knowing black history in order to understand America's present state:

> *I think that the past is all that makes the present coherent, and further, that the past will remain horrible for exactly as long as we refuse to assess it honestly.*

Laid out in brass letters, the quotes are submerged in the fountain. Water cascades over Baldwin's statement, agitated and shifting, then runs into a basin of calm water where Douglass's uplifting words are featured. Visitors can view themselves in the mirroring waters and in relation to these timeless thoughts. These powerful statements offer a preview of the Museum's core mission as the public crosses the final threshold into the central Heritage Hall.

BLACK & GREEN

The creation of a visually striking museum that made sustainability its centerpiece was a primary goal of Director Bunch's vision for the National Museum of African American History and Culture. Efficient energy and water use and waste disposal became integral to the architectural team's philosophy. Both the exterior and interior take advantage of passive design strategies to reduce the need for heating and cooling. Sustainability embraces the black American ethos of making good use of what is at hand—like the ingredients in a pot of gumbo or the colorful panels of reused fabric in quilts. To achieve the U.S. Green Building Council's LEED Gold certification, water, air, lighting, and waste systems needed to be meticulously planned.

Sunlight through the Corona panels casting shadows on the walls of the west side of the Museum at the main escalators. The panel openings control optimum heat gain and cooling in the interior.

The Museum has a wealth of innovative sustainable features. Many of the exterior building materials and interior finishes are made from recycled or recyclable materials. In keeping with the philosophy of sourcing locally, the architects and designers promoted the use of materials that could be found within a five-hundred-mile radius.

The project's civil engineers, Rummel, Klepper & Kahl, and the mechanical engineers, the WSP Group, in collaboration with landscape designers Gustafson Guthrie Nichol and the landscape architects of Smithsonian Gardens, incorporated many sustainable features. On the south side, for example, a large cistern placed belowground collects rain water, including water from the Porch's sloping roof. The water stored in the cistern as well as water diverted from sinks inside the Museum, known as gray water, is used for the irrigation of plants, for the large fountain in the South Plaza, and to flush toilets and urinals. To reduce water use, the bathrooms all use low-flow water closets, ultra-low-flow urinals, and low-flow faucets. A second container, a large storm-water vault on the west side, collects storm-water run-off. This holding tank slows the rate at which water enters the city's storm-water system to prevent floods in this, the lowest area of Constitution Avenue.

Efficient use of energy was another important goal. The Corona's panels provide an extra layer of protection against direct heat gain in summer and heat loss in winter, and day lighting in public and administrative zones reduces the need for artificial light. The architects and engineers divided the building into thermal zones within the stacking volumes to allow staff to control climate according to need, especially in galleries with sensitive artifacts. To reduce the cost of heating and cooling a very large building, heat pumps use the earth as a heat sink in summer.

Having 60 percent of the building belowground reduces its exposure to climate and diminishes the demand for energy. The layers of soil and plants provide a natural thermal barrier that keeps the History Galleries below from getting too hot in summer or too cold in winter. Two green roofs have been integrated into the building's design. One stretches over the large expanse of the underground History Galleries on the north side. Another green roof covers the Porch and provides thermal cooling in summer. On the main roof of the Museum, photovoltaic solar panels provide electricity to heat the building's water. Because much of the heating and cooling system is belowground, the roof becomes an uncluttered fifth façade, seen by those looking down from the top of the Washington Monument.

One of the most ingenious features of the Porch is how its cantilevered shading device and the pool create a microclimate that lowers the area's temperature five to ten degrees during the hot summer months. The carefully selected sassafras, katsura, ginkgo, white fringe, and cherry trees in the South Plaza also contribute to the microclimate's cooling effect.

Looking down from the Washington Monument onto the Museum's roof and its photovoltaic solar panels, which provide electricity to heat the building's water.

CHAPTER 7
INSIDE THE AFRICAN
AMERICAN STORY

"Most museums are based on the palace model, the great house where people come into a fantastic room, usually a void with staircases going up to grand rooms," David Adjaye explains. At the National Museum of African American History and Culture, the entrance establishes the reverse. "You come into a series of experiences. The central Heritage Hall is a space that feels neither inside nor outside because of the vast glass walls. It's like being underneath a canopy, under a structure, or under a tree." When visitors walk into the sunlit, spacious Heritage Hall, they enter a metaphorical clearing, the community gathering space of the hush harbor. The floor-to-ceiling windows lining the perimeter offer a panoramic view of the Museum's grounds.

Adjaye envisioned that the transparency and openness of this main space would draw the outside into the Museum and immerse the public in "the deep spatial memory of the forest." The Heritage Hall's precise geometric sightlines direct the view outward. Its polished floors and black perforated-metal ceiling, whose lighting recalls stars in the night sky, compress the overall feeling of the space. Because the ceiling tapers upward from the center, it sends visitors to the perimeter zones to access stairs and escalators. The heart of the Museum, the Heritage Hall can accommodate up to thirteen thousand people per day.

Architectural rendering of the oxidized-steel spiral stair that connects the Heritage Hall to the Concourse level.

Architectural rendering of the Heritage Hall, where visitors can find information on exhibitions or events while viewing public displays of artworks.

Whether entering the Museum through the Porch on the main south entrance or through the north entrance, visitors cross a series of threshold spaces. The perimeter threshold zone, twenty-five feet wide, wraps around the entire entry level and provides a unique perspective on the Corona's height and stepped glass curtain wall. At the north entrance, a bridge spans the Concourse level to offer a spectacular multistory view of the lower-level entrance to the History Galleries. The perimeter zone contains security checkpoints, escalators, the grand staircase to the Concourse level, the gift shop, an employees' entrance, and the coat and bag check area. Glass railings along the public stairs and balconies enhance the feelings of expansiveness and transparency throughout the Museum.

Four large pillars at the corners of the Heritage Hall house the public, freight, and employee elevators, along with other vital services such as emergency egress stairs and mechanical shafts. The architects wanted the Heritage Hall to be uncluttered by columns in order to create a wide-open space in which individuals and groups can easily determine where to get information, leave their belongings, and find the way toward their desired destination in the Museum. Between the two east pillars are the distinctive curved walls of the Corona Pavilion Theater, a space seating forty people. During the day, its engaging video presentation introduces the Museum's core themes; in the evenings, it hosts small-scale poetry readings, book discussions, and musical performances. The public can request information brochures and maps of the Museum from the large information desk strategically placed on the west side of the Heritage Hall on the way to the escalators.

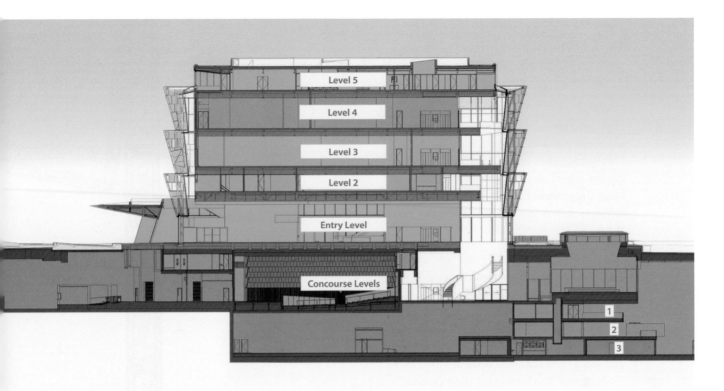

Architectural section drawing through the Museum, revealing the distribution of galleries and public spaces from the lowest levels to the upper floors, 2014. Visitors arrive at the Museum on the entry level, which houses the Heritage Hall, Orientation Theater, information desk, and museum shop. From here, they can descend one floor to the Concourse level, which contains the Contemplative Court, Oprah Winfrey Theater, Changing Exhibition Gallery, and Sweet Home Café, or they can proceed down two levels to the History Galleries on Sublevels One, Two, and Three. Upstairs from the entry level, visitors will find *Explore More!* (Level Two), Community Galleries (Level Three), and Culture Galleries (Level Four). Level Five holds staff offices.

On the north side of the hall, visitors can descend a curved staircase constructed from distinctive oxidized steel. This unique spiral stair, with precast terrazzo treads, takes the public to the lower-level Concourse.

The Concourse is a breathtaking space that reaches several stories high along the perimeter zone on the north side. Light streams in through the upper-level Corona to cast changing patterns of dappled shade throughout the day. With its durable terrazzo floors, the Concourse serves as a busy thoroughfare. From here, the public can enter the multilevel History Galleries, attend an event at the Oprah Winfrey Theater, dine in the Sweet Home Café, or visit the Contemplative Court with its Oculus fountain. Visitors can also take the opportunity to visit the Changing Exhibition Gallery, which hosts exhibits on a range of historical and cultural topics.

Because height restrictions prohibited the addition of more building volume above-ground, the best way to accommodate Ralph Appelbaum Associates' design for the History Galleries was to place them belowground. Working in consultation with Robert Silman Associates, the engineers for the lower levels, and the Smithsonian's architects and engineers, FAB/S designed a deeper foundation to accommodate the multilevel exhibit. The Museum visible from the Mall thus became an elegant pavilion surrounded by trees and a lush garden.

However, this meant the excavation of the site became more expensive and complicated. From site studies and the environmental impact report, the architects and engineers knew they would have to manage water infiltration, not least because the water table at the site was only five feet below grade.

To excavate the initial sixty feet below grade, the construction crews used cranes to build a pile in self-hardening grout (PSHG) retention wall to minimize water infiltration through the support walls and expedite the excavation of the 1,600-foot site perimeter. The work crew removed some 300,000 cubic yards of soil. The final excavation extends ninety feet below grade. At its lowest level, where the History Galleries begin, the concrete foundation wall measures six feet thick and is embedded with a mesh of 2¼-inch-diameter steel reinforcement bars. These massive retention and foundation walls allowed the four hundred or more construction workers descending on the site on a typical day to execute the various phases of the building process.

An immense area, the lower levels house many of the Museum's important back-of-house functions as well as the main History Galleries. They contain the loading areas, support offices, and areas for storage, conservation, and preparation. The numerous heating and cooling units are also located here. The important functions that keep the building running smoothly throughout the year are literally buried out of sight.

Tower cranes and construction workers building the foundations and structural cores as the Museum rises out of the ground in the early phases of construction, 2014.

Public spaces on the Concourse level include the Oprah Winfrey Theater, a state-of-the-art venue designed by Shen Milson & Wilke, seating 345 people and hosting public lectures, panel discussions, and interviews. The large stage and excellent acoustics of the theater provide a superb environment for music, dance, film, and theatrical performances. As a nod to the Museum's signature Corona, two mini-tiers of small glass fiber reinforced gypsum (GFRG) Corona panels, painted silver, wrap around the room. Dark wood floors and vertical slatted panels located at eye level bring warmth to the space.

On the east side of the Concourse, visitors can visit the Sweet Home Café. The menu includes dishes that are influenced by African American cuisine. The light that floods in through several skylights adds to the warm, relaxed dining experience, while horizontal bands of copper planters and green foliage create a smart but welcoming setting.

The main exhibition space on the Concourse is the David M. Rubenstein History Galleries, one of the largest exhibition halls ever built for the Smithsonian. The Smithsonian's curators, working with exhibition designers from Ralph Appelbaum Associates, have choreographed a compelling narrative of black history, in an American and global context, in a soaring three-story space encompassing 44,000 square feet of exhibition space.

The History Galleries are divided into three sections: "Slavery and Freedom," "Defending Freedom, Defining Freedom: Era of Segregation 1876–1968," and "A Changing America: 1968 and Beyond," each brought to life with a sequence of immersive vignettes. On entering the galleries from the main Concourse, visitors view a multimedia introduction that explains the centrality of the black experience to American and world history. From here, visitors can take a staircase or elevator to the lower level of the galleries (and the year 1400) to learn about the Old World, before there was a Europe or Africa, and the commencement of transatlantic trade.

The History Galleries' lighting, display cases, wall texts and color, ceiling heights, acoustics, sound, video, tactile elements, and interactive technologies create a seamless experience that enhances the telling of its stories, helping to engage and challenge the public. The designers had to plan for artifacts that were quite small and others that were very large, such as the vintage Stearman biplane *The Spirit of Tuskegee*, an authentic training aircraft flown by the storied African American airmen of World War II. Suspended from the concrete ceiling, the several-ton airplane soars above the "Defending Freedom, Defining Freedom" exhibition, captivating visitors with its powerful story of valor.

"Slavery and Freedom" exhibits small but poignant items such as the Bible owned by rebel leader Nat Turner and the hymn book and shawl belonging to abolitionist Harriet Tubman. Also on display are objects and stories that place the African American story in a global context, such as artifacts from the *São José-Paquet de Africa*, a Portuguese slave ship that sank off the coast of Cape Town, South Africa, on its way to Brazil, with more than four hundred enslaved people on board. Another display shows

Architectural rendering of the multilevel David M. Rubenstein History Galleries. Landing Theaters provide visitors with time and space for reflection.

a bill of sale for a "16-year-old Negro girl" named Polly, who was sold for $600 in 1835, and on view elsewhere are iron shackles once used to subdue a child and shackles used to restrain enslaved people aboard ships during the Middle Passage. These displays show the international nature of the slave trade and how it enriched Europe and the United States.

Some acquisitions are so large that they had to be installed before the upper levels were constructed. Such objects bring the aura of their former place into the Museum. The "Slavery and Freedom" exhibition, for example, contains an intact slave cabin from Point of Pines on Edisto Island, off the coast of Charleston, South Carolina. The yellow pine-framed structure, with its deep eave that overhangs the porch, allows visitors to connect to the life and work of the enslaved residents. In seeing the cabin's crude, unfinished materials and the cramped conditions in which an entire family lived, visitors witness both the harsh lives that enslaved men, women, and children endured and how community emerged from shared hardships.

At transition points between the galleries, Landing Theaters provide time and space for reflection and to learn more about the next series of displays. This ability to look backward and forward offers a fresh perspective on history, which Adjaye describes as "a modern way of looking at the world, to see it all at the same time." Located on the

Architectural rendering of interactive touch-screen displays in the History Galleries.

main level of each gallery, Reflection Booths allow individuals or small groups to share their personal stories inspired by the exhibitions. Quotes on the towering walls of the History Galleries, such as one from the activist Ida B. Wells—"The way to right wrongs is to turn the light of truth upon them"—offer inspiration and wisdom to visitors. In these interim spaces, Director Bunch wants patrons to "wrestle with the ambiguity of freedom" that black Americans experienced in all aspects of individual, family, and community life.

"Defending Freedom, Defining Freedom," the second section in the History Galleries, explores the years after the end of Reconstruction, examining how the nation struggled to define the status of African Americans. This represents a critical era for the United States and captures the tensions of the time—would African Americans gain full citizenship rights after more than 250 years of enslavement? Posters, broadsides from major civil rights actions, and shards from the shattered stained-glass windows of Birmingham's Sixteenth Street Baptist Church, bombed by white supremacists, bear witness to major aspects of the struggle and illustrate how African Americans not only survived huge challenges, but also carved out an important role for themselves in the nation. The exhibition illustrates how the United States changed as a consequence of the struggles and finally complied with its values of freedom, equality, and democracy.

Rendering of "Defending Freedom, Defining Freedom: Era of Segregation 1876–1968," with exhibits on the struggles and triumphs of the civil rights era. *Following pages:* Rendering of a restored ninety-year-old segregated Southern Railway car sitting near a cast-concrete guard tower from the Louisiana State Penitentiary in the "Defending Freedom, Defining Freedom" exhibit. Both the train railcar and the tower had to be installed onsite before the Museum walls were in place.

For "Defending Freedom, Defining Freedom," Bunch and his resourceful team of curators acquired a restored ninety-year-old Southern Railway car, which had to be brought up to the site after excavation, before the Museum walls were in place. Manufactured by the Pullman Palace Car Company in 1922, the passenger car was refurbished in 1940 (and again in 1952), with spacious accommodations for white patrons separated from the cramped seats for "colored" travelers. As visitors walk through and around the seventy-seven-ton car and view artifacts from the lives of Pullman porters, they get an insight into how racial restrictions impacted the minutiae of daily life.

"Defending Freedom, Defining Freedom" also features a twenty-one-foot cast-concrete guard tower that once surveyed the grounds of the maximum-security Louisiana State Penitentiary, also known as Angola Prison. The prison was built in the late 1800s on former plantations, and slave cabins provided its first jail cells. Leased out for backbreaking unpaid work, its black prisoners lived in a way that was very similar to enslavement. The juxtaposition of the train railcar, a mode of travel, and the prison, a space of confinement, is intended to show the degree to which legal segregation created separate but also interdependent black and white worlds. These places of memory are

difficult because they expose stories of cruelty, violence, and unfairness. Such realities of American life are often unseen and unspoken in historical narratives.

Visitors enter "A Changing America," the last of the three History Galleries, via a ramp from the exhibition on the era of segregation. The exhibition explores contemporary black life through stories about the social, economic, political, and cultural experiences of African Americans during the years from the death of Martin Luther King Jr. to the second election of Barack Obama. Its coverage is broad, stretching from the Black Arts Movement to hip-hop, from the Black Panthers to Obama's "Yes We Can" slogan for the 2008 presidential campaign, and from "Black is Beautiful" to #BlackLivesMatter. The exhibition also considers the challenges faced by African Americans—complicated by issues of immigration, class, and gender—as they continue to seek racial equality and social justice. Among the artifacts on display are a thirty-two-foot plywood mural from Resurrection City, the encampment set up on the National Mall during the 1968 Poor People's Campaign; the iconic poster of Black Panther leader Huey Newton holding a shotgun and a spear; a Vietnam veteran's "tour" jacket with black power insignia; Shirley Chisholm's 1972 presidential campaign buttons; and publications by Sonia Sanchez and Alice Walker. Also displayed are the façade of a brick doorway from Baxter Terrace Housing Project in Newark, New Jersey; Radio Raheem's boombox from the Spike Lee film *Do the Right Thing*; and a Coast Guard rescue basket used during Hurricane Katrina. Here, too, is the dress designed by Tracy Reese and worn by First Lady Michelle Obama in connection with the fiftieth anniversary of the March on Washington.

Exiting the exhibition, visitors find themselves on the Concourse, with easy access to the Contemplative Court, the Oprah Winfrey Theater, the Changing Exhibition Gallery, and the Sweet Home Café.

Near the history exhibitions, visitors discover the Contemplative Court, a peaceful sanctuary for reflection, before continuing to the galleries on the third and fourth levels. Perforated copper enclosed between two layers of glass provides privacy on all four sides, while light streams in through the large, circular clerestory window of the Oculus. (The exterior of the Oculus projects into the Museum's garden near the north entrance.) At the center of the court, granite benches surround a shallow, square pool into which water gently falls from above, its muffled sound amplifying the meditative atmosphere of the place.

Opposite, top: Reflection Booth in the "Slavery and Freedom" exhibit, where individuals and groups can share personal stories inspired by the displays. *Bottom*: Architectural rendering of the Contemplative Court, with its clerestory Oculus fountain, which provides visitors with a sanctuary for reflection.

CELEBRATING COMMUNITY & CULTURE

Escalators on the west and north sides of the Heritage Hall lead to the Community and Culture Galleries and the Resource Center, on the upper three levels. As the escalators ascend, a glance upward through the Corona's filigree panels, which create patterns of light and shadow below, reveals glimpses of the city. Moving from the center of the building to the perimeter gives a sense of the basic parti, or big idea, of the building: a series of nested boxes. In his early sketches, David Adjaye nested the upper galleries inside the Corona like a matryoshka, or Russian nesting doll, the artifacts in the galleries forming a dense center held by the glass curtain wall and the Corona.

The Museum adheres to the Smithsonian's core mission to increase as well as diffuse knowledge and devotes the second level to educational programs, study, and research. Visitors and researchers can use the Library by appointment to access primary and scholarly resources. It has a reading room with computer stations, stack space for eleven thousand volumes, and a display case for rotating exhibits of library and archival materials. They can also use the Explore Your Family History Center to discover resources related to family history, including the Freedmen's Bureau Archives and U.S. Census records. Guidance on how to conduct genealogical research is provided.

Washington Monument, as seen from the Lens in the third-level Community Gallery exhibition "Double Victory: The African American Military Experience."

This part of the Museum is also home to the Earl and Amanda Stafford Center for African American Media Arts (CAAMA), a research facility devoted to new scholarship and innovative applications in the fields of photography and new media by and about African Americans. Visitors can view CAAMA's research into the imagery of black Americans and other projects in its own exhibition space. Also on this level are the Target Learning Center Interactive Gallery and Classrooms' educational programs for families and schoolchildren. The Museum's education department has developed innovative programs, teaching tools, and online resources for the many school parties that visit the Museum.

The Community Galleries on Level Three and the Culture Galleries on Level Four are divided into thematic exhibitions. Place and memory are recurring themes. The displays highlight the roles of religious institutions, places of play and leisure, sites of work and entrepreneurship, home life and community, and arts venues. Sound, video, and interactive media help make the interpretive histories an immersive experience. Visitors can explore the challenges that racism imposed on the public and private lives of black Americans and the myriad ways in which they fought to overcome these obstacles.

The introductory Community Galleries exhibition, "Making a Way Out of No Way," highlights the formal and informal institutions and social organizations active in the African American struggle for change. The curators assembled a wealth of objects and stories that relate the joys and struggles in the lives of ordinary black Americans. The exhibition plumbs the history of the black press, educational institutions, religious organizations, businesses, unions, and activist organizations to reveal how African Americans fought to improve conditions for themselves and all Americans. Visitors can see the desks, stove, and sign from the Hope School, built in Pomaria, South Carolina, in 1925, and learn about philanthropic organizations

Design rendering of the third-level Community Gallery exhibition "Making a Way Out of No Way," with displays on the institutions and social organizations active in the African American struggle for change.

Rendering of the Community Gallery exhibit "Sports: Leveling the Playing Field," which delves into the struggles and triumphs of black athletes.

such as the Rosenwald Foundation, which collaborated with local communities to found thousands of such schools for black students in the South.

"Tradition of Activism" focuses on organizations such as the National Association of Colored Women, whose banner proclaims "Lifting as We Climb," and on the importance of the black press in informing the public. Magazines such as the National Association for the Advancement of Colored People's *Crisis* reported on boycotts and protests inspired by racially motivated discrimination and violence, while the *Chicago Defender* campaigned against segregation. Everyday objects such as lunchboxes and work uniforms tell the stories of how men and women fought for respect, decent working conditions, and fair wages in their everyday lives.

The Community Galleries also host the dynamic exhibition "Sports: Leveling the Playing Field," tracing the role of sports in African American culture and documenting the struggles and triumphs of black sportsmen and -women. Baseball, football, tennis, basketball, boxing, golf, and the Olympics were among the first sports in the nation to accept African Americans as equals. Sports became an important vehicle for social change. Photographs, newsreels, and magazines document their rise and recall the barnstorming Negro Leagues, which operated from 1920 to ca. 1960. Among the artifacts are the tennis racket that helped Althea Gibson win the Wimbledon tournament in 1957

Rendering of the "Power of Place" exhibition, at the center of the Community Galleries, which addresses the importance of place and region in the African American story.

and the historic *Time* magazine cover of 1947 featuring baseball great Jackie Robinson, whose signing by the Brooklyn Dodgers ended segregation in Major League Baseball.

On the other side of the Community Galleries, "Double Victory: The African American Military Experience" explores how African Americans' service in the military has opened up opportunities for the greater community and profoundly shaped the nation. The gallery explores the history of African American military service from the American Revolution to the War on Terror, and thematic sections explore topics such as African American recipients of the Medal of Honor. Near the entrance of the gallery is a metal-and-glass "Double V" apex, signifying the World War II Double Victory Campaign, which called for victory against fascism abroad and victory for equal rights at home. The Double V apex features large images of war and homefront scenes and patriotic, and often poignant, quotations. Visitors depart the gallery with an understanding that African Americans fought for dual victories long before the Double V Campaign: one for victory on the battlefields and one for liberty and equality in society.

"The Power of Place" exhibition, at the center of the Community Galleries, addresses the importance of place and region in the African American story. The curators and designers have created an array of intimately captured places from all over the United States, including a farm, a southern town, a northern city during the Great Migration, communities in the West, Louisiana State Penitentiary, and the African American leisure enclave at Oak Bluffs on Martha's Vineyard, Massachusetts. The exhibition documents the power and impact of the *Chicago Defender* newspaper in building Chicago, the spirit of entrepreneurship in Mae Reeves's Philadelphia hat shop, and the birth of hip-hop in the Bronx. It also explores race riots against African American towns and neighborhoods,

such as the Tulsa race riot of 1921. While the exhibition acknowledges that place is about geography, it recognizes that it is also about migration, memory, and emotion, and it invites visitors to think about the places they carry with them and the places they've left behind. Visitors can contribute their own personal stories of place through an interactive digital display.

Level Four is home to the Culture Galleries, featuring theater, music, visual arts, and other forms of cultural expression in four intersecting spaces that reflect the cross-pollination of cultural forms. Interactive exhibits explore the formation and transformation of black cultural identity, including the impact that racialized ideas of beauty and selfhood have had. The introductory "Cultural Expressions" exhibition draws out the connections among the exhibitions, animating the visitor experience.

Black traditional practices related to food, language, artistry, movement, and style fill an outer ring of the "Cultural Expressions" exhibition. On display is a sculpted wooden veranda post by Olowe of Ise, the Yoruban artist whose work helped inspire the form of the Museum building, and ironwork by Charleston blacksmith Philip Simmons, whose wrought ironwork influenced the Corona's filigree pattern. An interactive exhibition explores the written and spoken word, styles of dress, social dance and gestures, and the origins of black cuisine. An inner ring looks at similar practices in other cultures of the African Diaspora, including Mexico, Haiti, Barbados, and Cuba.

Moving into the "Musical Crossroads" exhibition, visitors can trace the evolution of African American music. Africans retained memories of the rhythms, style, and techniques of their homelands when they created new musical expressions that formed the foundations of modern American music. Interactive exhibits and media performances invite visitors to hear and see this history unfold. By sifting through the myriad styles and traditions—blues, spirituals, jazz, rhythm and blues, and classical, to name a few—visitors discover how African American music transformed genres and spurred innovation. Among the items on display are the dress worn by Marian Anderson for her historic concert on the steps of the Lincoln Memorial in 1939, the piano played by father of gospel Tommy Dorsey at the Pilgrim Baptist Church in Chicago, and Chuck Berry's red Cadillac, driven onstage at the Fox Theatre in St. Louis, the same theater that had turned him away as a child because he was black. The "Neighborhood Record Store" forms a communal space where visitors can share their musical interests.

The nearby "Taking the Stage" exhibition focuses on African American achievements in theater, film, and television. Costumes, posters, playbills, and scripts tell how African Americans have enriched American culture and used their talents as platforms for social change. Artifacts range from an 1857 broadside for a performance by the celebrated Shakespearean actor Ira Aldridge to a green velvet dress worn by singer Lena Horne in

Rendering of the Level Four "Cultural Expressions" exhibition, which explores traditional African American practices related to food, language, artistry, movement, and style.

the 1943 movie *Stormy Weather* and costumes worn by Sherman Hemsley and Isabel Sanford in the hit 1970s sitcom *The Jeffersons*. Along with moving accounts of the barriers that black Americans confronted in the entertainment industry, the exhibition highlights efforts by black independent filmmakers and theater artists to bring positive and diverse accounts of the experiences of African Americans to the stage and screen.

In the "Visual Arts and the American Experience" gallery, paintings, drawings, and sculptures highlight the diversity of the African American experience and open an artistic window onto the changing landscapes of life in America over the past two hundred years. Historical, social, and political interpretations seen elsewhere in the Museum help contextualize the art on view, and multimedia platforms offer new ways to engage with the material. The curators have grouped the works by aesthetic and intellectual criteria, so that the New Negro artistic movement of the 1920s is set in the context of the black cultural renaissance in Chicago, and the cultural militancy of the Black Arts Movement of the 1960s is expressed in various media. As visitors tour the unparalleled collection of American art, they can see how the curators have redefined the "African American art" moniker that once separated and confined artists and their works.

In line with Lonnie Bunch's desire to root the history told inside the Museum in the context of Washington, D.C., the city is given a prominent role in describing the African American experience, both as the nation's capital and as the home of many African Americans. Lens spaces on each of the upper-level galleries look out onto the city, reminding visitors that landscapes are essential to the telling of history and that the untold history of African Americans can be found in many places and spaces. Large, passage-like windows that peek through the screen of the Corona allow visitors to look out on the Washington Monument, the Lincoln Memorial, the White House, Federal Triangle, the National Mall, the U.S. Capitol, and the city of Washington, D.C., itself. They resonate with the history told in the galleries. In the "Defending Freedom, Defining Freedom" gallery, for example, schoolchildren learn about the story of the 1963 March on Washington for Jobs and Freedom, when Martin Luther King Jr. delivered his famous "I Have a Dream" speech on the steps of the Lincoln Memorial. In an upper-level Lens of the "Double Victory" exhibition, that school group can look west to the Lincoln Memorial. The Medal of Honor Hall in the same Lens space catalogues African American recipients of the nation's highest military honor for valor. Its location connects the history of African American military personnel to the monument to President Abraham Lincoln, who authorized the resolution establishing the first Navy Medal of Honor in 1861 during the Civil War. These vistas fulfill Bunch's mandate that the Museum use "African American history and culture as a lens onto what it means to be an American."

Opposite, top: Rendering of the "Taking the Stage" exhibition, where visitors can see artifacts from and recorded performances by African American artists who used their talents as platforms for social change. *Bottom:* The paintings, drawings, and sculptures in the fourth-level "Visual Arts and the American Experience" exhibition highlight the diversity of the African American experience. The design rendering shows how visitors can use hand-held devices to access in-depth descriptions of artworks and artists.

CONCLUSION

On September 24, 2016, President Barack Obama cut the ribbon that inaugurated the opening of the National Museum of African American History and Culture. Since the Museum opened its doors, thousands of people of all ages have converged on the new building to learn about black culture and its place in America's history. All those involved in its creation and those who currently work in its various departments are immensely proud of their new building. A monument to human resilience and determination, the Museum has taken up its place along America's public commons, the National Mall. Local residents, groups from elsewhere in the United States, and visitors from around the world have a new must-see destination.

Revealing the "truth about America," as James Baldwin once said, is not a short-term commitment for Director Lonnie Bunch. He believes that the new Museum elevates black history and culture to a new level. It "embraces a more holistic and diverse view of the African American experience of 'race' in America, a level that recognizes that new paradigms and new strategies have to shape both the product and the process of exploring 'race' in museums."

For audiences of all ages, the new Museum opens fresh perspectives on how America remembers its past. The National Museum of African American History and Culture will continue to develop new exhibitions and public programs that show how the inequalities and injustices endured by black Americans have clashed with the nation's noble aspirations to equality and fairness. But this progress is ongoing today. The new Museum actively contributes to the public conversation about what the nation's future holds for its citizens. As the Museum evolves the content of its exhibitions and programs, the interior of its building will also evolve in order to accommodate new needs and changing audiences.

The National Museum of African American History and Culture creates a place for people from around the globe to better understand America's past, which can help everyone aspire to a more just and equitable world. It is a place where everyone can engage in the many different and complicated dimensions of America; it is a place where, in the words of the Museum's vision statement, "all Americans remember" and where a dialogue about race can happen that fosters "a spirit of healing and reconciliation." The Museum demonstrates how African Americans have made the country work toward fulfilling its promise of equality, freedom, justice, and democracy, and in telling this story, the Museum continues with this charge to make America better for everyone.

Corner of the Corona, whose angles echo the canted sides of the pyramid atop the Washington Monument.

INDEX

PHOTO CREDITS

Key: top (*t*), bottom (*b*), left (*l*), right (*r*), center (*c*)

National Museum of African American History and Culture: 2: Alan Karchmer/NMAAHC **5:** Alan Karchmer/ NMAAHC **7:** Photograph by Martin Stupich **8:** Alan Karchmer/NMAAHC **11:** Alan Karchmer/NMAAHC **12–13:** Alan Karchmer/NMAAHC **14:** Alan Karchmer/NMAAHC **15:** Alan Karchmer/NMAAHC **27:** *b* 2016.74, Collection of the Smithsonian National Museum of African American History and Culture, Gift from the Ball-Haagland family in memory of Robert Ball **29:** 2015.178, Collection of the Smithsonian National Museum of African American History and Culture, Gift of Ingrid Rose in memory of Milton M. Rose **46:** Site Evaluation Study prepared by Plexus Scientific Corporation and Page Southerland Page, Inc. **47:** Site Evaluation Study prepared by Plexus Scientific Corporation and Page Southerland Page, Inc. **48:** Freelon Adjaye Bond/SmithGroup **56:** *t* Diller Scofidio + Renfro *c* Foster + Partners *b* Devrouax & Purnell Architects/Planners and Pei Cobb Freed & Partners Architects **57:** *t* Moody Nolan in association with Antoine Predock Architect *b* Moshe Safdie and Associates & Sultan Campbell Britt and Associates **58:** Michael Barnes/Smithsonian Institution **60:** Courtesy of David Adjaye Associates © David Adjaye **64–65:** Freelon Adjaye Bond/ SmithGroup **67:** *t* Freelon Adjaye Bond/SmithGroup *b* © 2010 Judy Davis/Hoachlander Davis Photography, LLC Washington DC USA Ph: 202/364-9306 All Rights Reserved. **68:** *t, b* Donald Hurlburt/Smithsonian Institution **72:** Alan Karchmer/NMAAHC **77:** Freelon Adjaye Bond/SmithGroup **78:** Alan Karchmer/NMAAHC **80:** *t, b* Courtesy of David Adjaye Associates © David Adjaye **83:** Freelon Adjaye Bond/SmithGroup **84:** Michael Barnes/Smithsonian Institution **85:** Michael Barnes/Smithsonian Institution **86:** *tr, tl, br, bl* Alan Karchmer/NMAAHC **87:** 2016.41.1 **88–89:** Alan Karchmer/NMAAHC **90:** Alan Karchmer/NMAAHC **92:** Plexus Scientific Corporation and Page Southerland Page **94:** Alan Karchmer/NMAAHC **95:** *t, b* Design: Gustafson Guthrie Nichol **96:** Alan Karchmer/NMAAHC **97:** Alan Karchmer/NMAAHC **99:** Design: Gustafson Guthrie Nichol **100–101:** Alan Karchmer/NMAAHC **102:** Freelon Adjaye Bond/SmithGroup **106:** Freelon Adjaye Bond/SmithGroup **108:** Alan Karchmer/NMAAHC **111:** Alan Karchmer/ NMAAHC **112:** Freelon Adjaye Bond/SmithGroup **114:** Design: Ralph Appelbaum Associates **115:** Freelon Adjaye Bond/SmithGroup **116–117:** Blake Thompson, Clark Concrete Contractors, LLC **119:** Design: Ralph Appelbaum Associates **120:** Design: Ralph Appelbaum Associates **121:** Design: Ralph Appelbaum Associates **122–123:** Design: Ralph Appelbaum Associates **125:** *t* Design: Ralph Appelbaum Associates *b* Freelon Adjaye Bond/SmithGroup **126:** Alan Karchmer/NMAAHC **128–129:** Design: Ralph Appelbaum Associates **130:** Design: Ralph Appelbaum Associates **131:** Design: Ralph Appelbaum Associates **132:** Design: Ralph Appelbaum Associates **135:** Design: Ralph Appelbaum Associates **136:** Alan Karchmer/NMAAHC

Alamy: 53: *b* © Danita Delimont / Alamy Stock Photo. **Bridgeman Images: 75:** *br A Plantation Burial*, 1860 (oil on canvas), Antrobus, John (1837–1907) / The Historic New Orleans Collection / Bridgeman Images. **81:** Yoruba veranda post, Nigeria (wood), Olowe of Ise (c. 1875–1938) / Museum Fünf Kontinente, Staatliche Museen in Bayern, Munich, Germany / Photo © Heini Schneebli / Bridgeman Images. **DuSable Museum: 32:** *bl* DuSable Museum of African American History, Chicago, Illinois. **Getty Images: 24:** Photo by Hulton Archive / Getty Images **35:** *t* Photo by Lawrence K. Ho / *Los Angeles Times* via Getty Images *br* Photo by Paul Marotta / Getty Images **38:** *tl* Bettmann Archive / Getty Images **42:** *t* Photo by Paul Morse / White House via Getty Images **52:** *t* Richard Lautens / *Toronto Star* via Getty Images. **Library of Congress: 20:** Library of Congress (LC-DIG-det-4a12513) **22:** *t* Library of Congress (LC-DIG-ggbain-50141) **36:** Library of Congress (HABS DC-141-17) **104:** *t* Library of Congress (LC-DIG-ppmsca-08755) **105:** *b* Library of Congress (LC-DIG-fsa-8b32787). **National Afro-American Museum and Cultural Center: 34:** *b* Courtesy of the National Afro-American Museum and Cultural Center. **National Park Service: 45:** *b* National Capitol Planning Commission. **New York Public Library: 30:** From The New York Public Library / Schomburg Center for Research in Black Culture, Photographs and Prints Division **32:** *tr* From The New York Public Library / Schomburg Center for Research in Black Culture, Photographs and Prints Division **45:** *t* From The New York Public Library / Lionel Pincus and Princess Firyal Map Division. **Philip Simmons Foundation: 82:** *tr* Reprinted with permission from the Philip Simmons Foundation, Inc., photographed by Claire Y. Greene (1958–2006) 1992. **Public domain: 27:** *t* From *The Crisis* (December 1913): 79. **Redux Pictures: 59:** *t* Fred R. Conrad / *New York Times*. **Smithsonian Institution Archives: 33:** *t* OPA-1067-06. **39:** *t* SIA 2016-009507. **United States Holocaust Memorial Museum: 54:** *t* Timothy Hursley

For permission to reproduce illustrations appearing in this book, please correspond directly with the owners of the works, as seen above. Smithsonian Books does not retain reproduction rights for these images individually or maintain a file of addresses for sources.

ACKNOWLEDGMENTS

From the Author

I owe a debt of gratitude to all those who contributed their knowledge and experience to the creation and construction of the Smithsonian's National Museum of African American History and Culture. There were many, but I particularly thank those who graciously met with me for interviews, including, from the museum, Founding Director Lonnie G. Bunch III, Deputy Director Kinshasha Holman Conwill, Scholarly Advisory Committee member Deborah Willis, and other staff members who provided documents and information. Architects David Adjaye, Philip Freelon, Zena Howard, Kathryn Gustafson, and Peter Cook and engineer Guy Nordenson offered detailed perspectives on the design and construction process. The Smithsonian Institution's Derek Ross, Brenda Sanchez, Sharon Park, Amy Ballard, William Donnelly, Kendra L. Gastright, and the late Claudine K. Brown shared their invaluable insights. A special thank-you to Congressman John Lewis and his staff and to Judge Robert Wilkins for illuminating the history of the various public and private initiatives to create the museum. Thanks to my colleague Leslie Gill, who kindly read early drafts of the manuscript. And last, a word of thanks to Carolyn Gleason and the excellent staff at Smithsonian Books for their feedback and guidance. —*Mabel O. Wilson*

From the National Museum of African American History and Culture

We are deeply grateful to all who made this publication—and the museum's founding—possible. First and foremost, we thank our author, Mabel O. Wilson, for her eloquent words and keen observations. She has woven an extraordinarily rich narrative of the century-long road that led to the realization of this building and the dreams that it houses.

The entire process of designing and building the museum would not have been possible without two principal members of the Consulting Parties, the Commission of Fine Arts (CFA) and the National Capital Planning Commission (NCPC). Their guidance and insights were invaluable. As with all of our architectural work, we also thank our colleagues at the Smithsonian who have dedicated years of their time and talent as our partners in this endeavor, especially our colleagues at Smithsonian Facilities: Derek Ross, Brenda Sanchez, Jud McIntire, Sharon Park, Jane Passman, Amy Ballard, Nancy Bechtol, Walter Ennaco, Debra Nauta-Rodriguez, Stephen Christensen, Ann Trowbridge, Dottie Leffler, Michael Bellamy, Curtis Davis, William Brubaker, and Bruce Kendall. Many colleagues, including Sheila P. Burke, Sheryl Kolasinski, and Harry Rombach, were integral at critical moments, from the earliest days of site selection to later junctures.

This building, this book, and so much of our work were animated by the sage advice of a number of our late colleagues, especially Evelyn S. Lieberman, Claudine K. Brown, and Clement Alexander Price. It is fitting that this publication draws its title from the words of one of America's great historians and the former chair of the museum's Scholarly Advisory Committee, the late John Hope Franklin. He and his colleagues were constants in shaping our efforts. We also remember Ivan Smyntyna, who died in a tragic accident while helping to construct the museum and whose memory lives on in our work.

In addition, the Museum Council has been exemplary in their generosity and deep commitment. Their stalwart support has been unwavering and essential. We also thank the Regents of the Smithsonian Institution, current Secretary David J. Skorton, previous secretaries Lawrence M. Small and G. Wayne Clough, and Under Secretary Albert Horvath for making the building of this museum an institutional priority. We offer a very special word of thanks to Provost Richard Kurin for his singular and steadfast leadership and advocacy.

Smithsonian Books guided us in making this a publication of which we are enormously proud. Our colleagues at the museum—Lynn Chase, Laura Coyle, Michèle Gates Moresi, Joanne Hyppolite, Douglas Remley, Bryan Sieling, Michelle Joan Wilkinson, and Renee Anderson—are owed particular thanks for their tireless work and contributions to the foundations of this book. Finally, the exquisite photography of Alan Karchmer illuminates the pages of this book in astonishing ways. —*Kinshasha Holman Conwill*

Presidential Commission
Robert L. Wright, Chair
Claudine K. Brown, Vice Chair
Senator Sam Brownback
Senator Max Cleland
Congressman John Lewis
Congressman J. C. Watts Jr.
Henry L. Aaron
Renee Amoore
Vicky A. Bailey
Currie D. Ballard
Lerone Bennett Jr.
Robert W. Bogle
Howard Dodson
John E. Fleming
Barbara Franco
Michael L. Lomax
Andrew G. McLemore Jr.
Eric L. Sexton
Harold K. Skramstad Jr.
Beverly J. Caruthers Thompson
Cicely Tyson
Robert L. Wilkins

Smithsonian Secretaries
David J. Skorton
G. Wayne Clough
Lawrence M. Small

Smithsonian Regents 2016
Chief Justice John G. Roberts Jr.,
  Chancellor
Vice President Joseph R. Biden Jr.
John W. McCarter Jr., Chair
Shirley Ann Jackson, Vice Chair
Senator John Boozman
Senator Patrick J. Leahy
Senator David Perdue
Representative Xavier Becerra
Representative Tom Cole
Representative Sam Johnson
Barbara M. Barrett
Steve Case
John Fahey
Robert P. Kogod
Risa J. Lavizzo-Mourey
Michael M. Lynton
David M. Rubenstein

Museum Council 2016
Richard D. Parsons, Co-Chair
Linda Johnson Rice, Co-Chair
Representative Xavier Becerra
Willie L. Brown Jr.
Laura W. Bush

James Ireland Cash Jr.
Kenneth Irvine Chenault
N. Anthony Coles
Brian C. Cornell
Ann Marie Fudge
Allan C. Golston
James A. Johnson
Robert L. Johnson
Quincy D. Jones
Ann Dibble Jordan
Michael L. Lomax
Brian T. Moynihan
Homer Alfred Neal
E. Stanley O'Neal
Samuel J. Palmisano
General Colin L. Powell
Franklin D. Raines
Ruth J. Simmons
David J. Skorton, Secretary
Patricia Q. Stonesifer
H. Patrick Swygert
Anthony Welters
Oprah Winfrey
Robert L. Wright

Scholarly Advisory Committee
John Hope Franklin, Founding
  Chairman
Michael Blakey
Taylor Branch
Johnetta Betsch Cole
Drew S. Days III
Leslie Fenwick
Alfred Moss
Richard Powell
Clement Alexander Price
Bernice Johnson Reagon
Alvia Wardlaw
Deborah Willis

Cooperating Agencies
Advisory Council on Historic
  Preservation
Commission of Fine Arts
DC Historic Preservation Office
National Capital Planning
  Commission
National Park Service

Predesign Team
Site Analysis
Freelon Bond
Page Southerland Page, Inc.
Plexus Scientific Corporation

Environmental Impact Statement
Louis Berger
Public Outreach
Justice & Sustainability Associates
Historic Preservation
Robinson & Associates, Inc.
Programming
Institution for Learning
  Innovation
Lord Cultural Resources

Design Team
Architecture
Freelon Adjaye Bond/SmithGroup
  The Freelon Group; Adjaye
  Associates; Davis Brody Bond;
  SmithGroupJJR
Landscape Architecture
Gustafson Guthrie Nichol
Structural Engineering
Robert Silman Associates
Guy Nordenson and Associates
*Mechanical Electrical Plumbing
and Fire Protection*
WSP Parsons Brinckerhoff
Civil Engineering
Rummel, Klepper & Kahl
Exhibition Design
Ralph Appelbaum Associates

Construction Team
Prime Contractor
Clark/Smoot/Russell
  Clark Construction Group, LLC
  Smoot Construction Company
  H. J. Russell & Company
Construction Manager
McKissack & McKissack
Corona
Enclos Corp.
Northstar Contracting, Inc.
Landscape
Rugo Stone, LLC
Ruppert Landscape
Structural
AIW, Inc./American Iron Works
Clark Concrete Contractors, LLC
SteelFab, Inc.
Electrical
Mona Electric Group, Inc.
Mechanical
Southland Industries
Exhibition Fabrication & Installation
D&P

This book may be purchased for educational, business, or sales promotional use. For information, please write: Special Markets Department, Smithsonian Books, P.O. Box 37012, MRC 513, Washington, DC 20013

Published by Smithsonian Books
Director: Carolyn Gleason
Managing Editor: Christina Wiginton
Assistant Editor: Laura Harger
Editorial Assistant: Jaime Schwender

NATIONAL MUSEUM OF AFRICAN AMERICAN HISTORY AND CULTURE
Director: Lonnie G. Bunch III
General Editor and Deputy Director: Kinshasha Holman Conwill
Publications Team: Michèle Gates Moresi, Laura Coyle, Douglas Remley
Architectural Photography: Alan Karchmer

Produced by Potomac Global Media in collaboration with Toucan Books, Ltd.
Kevin Mulroy, Publisher, Potomac Global Media, LLC; Ellen Dupont, Managing Director, Toucan Books, Ltd.; Dorothy Stannard, Editor; John Paine, Contributing Editor; Autumn Green, Abigail Mitchell, Assistant Editors; Dolores York, Proofreader; Nic Nicholas, Indexer; Kris Hanneman, Picture Research; Christine Vincent, Picture Manager; David Chickey, Art Direction & Design

Library of Congress Cataloging-in-Publication Data
Wilson, Mabel (Mabel O.), author. | Bunch, Lonnie G., writer of foreword
Begin with the past : Building the National Museum of African American History and Culture /
    Mabel O. Wilson; foreword by Lonnie G. Bunch III
Description: Washington, DC : Smithsonian Books, 2016
Identifiers: LCCN 2016015805 | ISBN 9781588345691 (hardback)
Subjects: LCSH: National Museum of African American History and Culture (U.S.) | Freelon Adjaye Bond/
    SmithGroup. | Museum architecture—Washington (D.C.) | Washington (D.C.)—Buildings, struc-
    tures, etc. | BISAC: ARCHITECTURE / Buildings / Landmarks & Monuments. | ARCHITECTURE /
    History / Contemporary (1945–).
Classification: LCC NA6700.W37 W55 2016 | DDC 720.9753—dc23 LC record available at
    https://lccn.loc.gov/2016015805

Manufactured in Canada, not at government expense
20 19 18 17 16   6 5 4 3 2